GENESIS to REVELATION

EZEKIEL
DANIEL

LINDA B. HINTON

GENESIS to REVELATION
EZEKIEL
DANIEL
LINDA B. HINTON

GENESIS TO REVELATION SERIES:
EZEKIEL, DANIEL
PARTICIPANT

Copyright © 1984 by Graded Press
Revised Edition Copyright © 1997 by Abingdon Press
Updated and Revised Edition Copyright © 2019 by Abingdon Press
All rights reserved.

No part of this work may be reproduced or transmitted in any form or by any means, electronic or mechanical, including photocopying and recording, or by any information or retrieval system, except as may be expressly permitted in the 1976 Copyright Act or in writing from the publisher. Requests for permission should be addressed in writing to Permissions, The United Methodist Publishing House, 2222 Rosa L. Parks Blvd., Nashville, TN 37228 or e-mailed to permissions@umpublishing.org.

All Scripture quotations, unless otherwise indicated, are taken from the Holy Bible, New International Version®, NIV®. Copyright ©1973, 1978, 1984, 2011 by Biblica, Inc.™ Used by permission of Zondervan. All rights reserved worldwide. www.zondervan.com The "NIV" and "New International Version" are trademarks registered in the United States Patent and Trademark Office by Biblica, Inc.™

Scripture quotations marked (NRSV) are taken from the New Revised Standard Version of the Bible, copyright 1989, Division of Christian Education of the National Council of the Churches of Christ in the United States of America. Used by permission. All rights reserved.

ISBN 9781501855764

Manufactured in the United States of America

19 20 21 22 23 24 25 26 27 28—10 9 8 7 6 5 4 3 2 1

ABINGDON PRESS
Nashville

TABLE OF CONTENTS

1. God Comes to Ezekiel (Ezekiel 1–5) 6

2. The Fate of Jerusalem (Ezekiel 6–11) 14

3. Faithlessness Brings Exile and Desolation (Ezekiel 12–15) 21

4. From God's Saving Acts to Grief (Ezekiel 16–19) 28

5. A History of Sin and Its Consequences (Ezekiel 20–24) 34

6. Prophecies Against the Nations (Ezekiel 25–28) 43

7. Prophecies Against Egypt (Ezekiel 29–32) 50

8. Restoration and Fulfillment (Ezekiel 33–39) 59

9. Vision of the Restored Temple (Ezekiel 40–44) 67

10. Vision of the Restored Land (Ezekiel 45–48) 74

11. God's Servants in Babylon (Daniel 1–4) 81

12. Human Destiny, Divine Control (Daniel 5–8) 88

13. The Time of the End (Daniel 9–12) 96

Glossary 105

While I was among the exiles by the Kebar River, the heavens were opened and I saw visions of God. (1:1)

GOD COMES TO EZEKIEL

Ezekiel 1–5

DIMENSION ONE: WHAT DOES THE BIBLE SAY?

Answer these questions by reading Ezekiel 1

1. When and where does Ezekiel have his vision of God? (1:1)

2. What three natural elements appear in Ezekiel's vision? (1:4)

3. What likeness appears from the midst of the vision? (1:5a)

4. What is the appearance of these creatures? (1:5b-6)

5. What are the four faces of each creature? (1:10)

6. What does Ezekiel see next to each creature? (1:15-16)

GOD COMES TO EZEKIEL

7. What does Ezekiel do when he sees the glory of the Lord? (1:28c)

Answer these questions by reading Ezekiel 2

8. What does the Lord call Ezekiel? (2:1)

9. Where does the Lord send Ezekiel? (2:3)

10. Why is Ezekiel sent? (2:3-4)

Answer these questions by reading Ezekiel 3

11. How is Ezekiel prepared to face the rebellious house of Israel? (3:8)

12. What four things is Ezekiel to do with God's words? (3:10-11)

13. How does the vision affect Ezekiel? (3:15)

14. Why does the Lord send Ezekiel to Israel? (3:21)

15. By whose power does Ezekiel speak? (3:27)

Answer these questions by reading Ezekiel 4

16. Why is Ezekiel told to portray, in miniature, Jerusalem under siege? (4:1-3)

17. How is Ezekiel to bear the punishment for Israel? For Judah? (4:4-6)

18. What is symbolized for Israel by Ezekiel baking his food on human excrement? (4:12-13)

19. What will the people of Jerusalem be forced to ration under their punishment? (4:16-17)

Answer these questions by reading Ezekiel 5

20. With what is Ezekiel to shave his head? (5:1)

21. What is Ezekiel to do with his shorn hair? (5:1-4)

22. What will the people of Israel learn from their punishment? (5:13)

DIMENSION TWO: WHAT DOES THE BIBLE MEAN?

■ **Background.** Nebuchadnezzar II (also spelled Nebuchadrezzar) was king of Babylon (605–562 BC). While still crown prince, he conducted military campaigns for his ailing father, Nabopolassar. In 605 BC, his armies defeated the Egyptians at Carchemish along the Euphrates River. He pursued the Egyptians to the frontiers of Egypt. All of Syria and Palestine then came under his influence. King Jehoiakim of Judah became one of his vassal kings.

The prophet Jeremiah believed Nebuchadnezzar to be God's instrument to punish unfaithful Judah (Jeremiah 25:1-11). Jeremiah's prophecy was rejected, and his life was threatened.

King Jehoiakim tried to rid himself of Babylonian influence after the Babylonians were defeated by the Egyptians in 601 BC. This was not a decisive defeat, however. In 599 BC, Nebuchadnezzar reasserted his dominance of the regions east of Syria and Palestine. In 598 BC, he directed his armies toward Judah.

The Babylonian army besieged Jerusalem in December of 598 BC. Jehoiakim was killed and his eighteen-year-old son, Jehoiachin, became king. He reigned for three months (see 2 Kings 24:8). According to the official annals of the Babylonian kings, the army of Nebuchadnezzar took Jerusalem on March 16, 597 BC. The king, his court, and about ten thousand scribes, soldiers, artisans, prophets, and priests were taken to Babylon. Ezekiel was in this group. Zedekiah, Jehoiachin's uncle, was given charge of Judah as puppet governor.

Five years after the deportation to Babylon, Ezekiel is thrust into his prophetic ministry by a dramatic vision. He will soon deliver a message to the people of Israel that will shatter their hopes of a quick return to power in their homeland.

■ **Ezekiel 1:1-3.** These verses introduce the Book of Ezekiel. "In my thirtieth year" may refer to Ezekiel's age at the time of his call. Or the phrase may refer to the time when the book was written, thirty years after Ezekiel's call. We cannot be certain of the exact meaning.

Based on a lunar calendar, with the beginning of the year in the spring, Ezekiel's vision came approximately on July 31, 593 BC.

Verses 2 and 3 may have been added by an editor. These verses clarify the dates of verse 1, establish Ezekiel's lineage, and elaborate on where he lived (see similar introductions to Jeremiah, Hosea, Joel, Jonah, Micah, Zephaniah, Haggai, and Zechariah).

The Kebar River was a canal branching from the Euphrates above Babylon and rejoining the Euphrates below Nippur. Some Jewish exiles settled near Nippur.

■ **Ezekiel 1:4.** The windstorm (1 Kings 19:11), an immense cloud (Exodus 19:16), and fire (1 Kings 19:11-12; Exodus 19:18) are associated with God's manifestation on earth.

■ **Ezekiel 1:5-14.** This section refers to four living creatures. These creatures are probably cherubim, guardians of sacred areas (see Genesis 3:24; Exodus 20:18-19; 1 Kings 6:23-28; Revelation 4:6).

■ **Ezekiel 1:15-25.** Here we read about a "wheel intersecting a wheel" ("wheel within a wheel" in the NRSV). Perhaps these wheels were located at right angles to each other and could move in any direction. The four faces may symbolize God's dominion and power over heaven and earth.

■ **Ezekiel 1:26-28.** The Hebrew word for glory is *kabod*. This term describes God's presence (Psalm 19:1; Isaiah 66:18). Ezekiel experiences God's complete power and holiness in God's *kabod*. For Ezekiel to encounter God's presence outside of Zion is unique. This encounter breaks into the prophet's old beliefs about God, and changes his life. God reveals a freedom to meet the people wherever they are.

■ **Ezekiel 2:1-7.** God calls Ezekiel *Ben-adam*. This name means "son of man," "human being, or "mortal." The term reminds Ezekiel of his lowliness compared to the glory of God. In verses 4-7, God gives Ezekiel his commission and the reason for his commission.

The *dabar* (word) of God is a living thing for Ezekiel. According to Genesis 1, the word of God has the power to create. According to Old Testament tradition, the creative power of God's word extends to the prophet's words as well. So the prophet proclaims, 'This is what the Sovereign LORD says." Ezekiel was to make known the word of God for the future.

■ **Ezekiel 2:8–3:3.** Eating the scroll is Ezekiel's ordination as a prophet. Verses 9 and 10 describe the scroll as containing

GOD COMES TO EZEKIEL

"words of lament and mourning and woe." These words symbolize Ezekiel's message to the people of Israel. Ezekiel is to speak only what God gives him to speak. Ezekiel eats the scroll and accepts his commission as God's witness.

- **Ezekiel 3:4-11.** Here God prepares Ezekiel for his mission to the people of Israel. Ezekiel is sent to "all the Israelites," not just to the Judean exiles.
- **Ezekiel 3:17-19.** These verses are found also in Ezekiel 33:7-9. They emphasize that Ezekiel must watch and warn because his message is one of life and death.
- **Ezekiel 3:22-27.** Ezekiel is summoned by God. In a similar way, Philip was summoned by God through an angel (see Acts 8:26-27).
- **Ezekiel 4:1-3.** Here God tells Ezekiel to take a block of clay and draw a map of Jerusalem on it. Clay was more common in Babylonia than in Palestine. Remember that Ezekiel received his visions while in Babylonia.
- **Ezekiel 4:4-8.** Ezekiel is to lie on his right side and left side a total of 430 days. This symbol of Israel's punishment corresponds to the years Israel spent in servitude in Egypt (Exodus 12:40). In his suffering, Ezekiel both represents and reveals Israel's guilt.
- **Ezekiel 4:9-16.** In these verses, God tells Ezekiel what to do about his food. God is saying that Ezekiel's food must reflect the coming siege of Jerusalem. Mixing different types of grains means that the siege will cause a lack of food in the city. Cooking on human excrement represents the unclean food (Deuteronomy 23:12-14) that will result from the siege.
- **Ezekiel 5:1-4.** The sword used as a razor represents military defeat for Israel. The fate of Ezekiel's shaved hair represents the fate of Jerusalem's citizens (v. 12).
- **Ezekiel 5:5-12.** Jerusalem, the center of the world, will be destroyed because of human rebelliousness (sin). This message of God's power and intentions is to all the world.

"Detestable practices" ("abominations" in the NRSV) comes from the Hebrew word to be abhorred. These are idolatrous practices or violations of custom (Daniel 11:31).

- **Ezekiel 5:13.** Here God says, "They will know that I the LORD have spoken." This statement is a key phrase and an important element in Ezekiel's message. The passage is saying that all God's actions should result in the people's knowledge of God. This new knowledge implies a call to new obedience.
- **Ezekiel 5:14-17.** The nations to whom Israel was to be a source of blessing (Genesis 12:1-3) are now to regard it with reproach and horror (Ezekiel 36:34; Jeremiah 24:9-10). The four plagues of verse 17 show the completeness of Israel's destruction (Ezekiel 14:21).

God demands complete loyalty from the people. Israel must pay for its disloyalty. The consequences of sin cannot be avoided.

DIMENSION THREE: WHAT DOES THE BIBLE MEAN TO ME?

Ezekiel 1:22-28—Learning of God

Ezekiel was reared in a priestly family and trained for the priesthood. His faith was grounded in Palestine and in God's presence in the Jerusalem Temple. Yet, he is in a foreign land without the Temple or the traditional priesthood. God confronts Ezekiel in Babylonia, and Ezekiel is overwhelmed. His view of the world, which had been secure, was being replaced, questioning the whole present condition of the chosen people. The one fixed point in Ezekiel's world was God. But God was demanding a total reorganization of the prophet's world.

Like Ezekiel and his listeners, we have much to learn about God. How do we react when we are confronted with new knowledge of God? Ezekiel felt bitter and overwhelmed. Other natural reactions might also include fear or confusion. When have your assumptions about God been shattered? What was your reaction at these times?

Ezekiel 3:14-16—Obedience to God

Ezekiel goes through a critical transformation between Ezekiel 3:14-15 and 3:16. We are given no details of that time when he sat overwhelmed for seven days, though this must have been an important time for him. Seven days is given as a period of mourning in Genesis 50:10.

When we are confronted with new knowledge of God, do we give ourselves time to absorb it? How might we unify the sometimes conflicting forces within us to set ourselves toward God's purposes?

Ezekiel 3:1-2; 4; 5:1-4—Word as Deed and Deed as Word

Ezekiel took on the word of God through physical, symbolic actions. These actions were part of his proclamation and preaching of God's word. Ezekiel took upon himself the guilt, terror, discomfort, and alienation that his people were to experience. As God's messenger, he was one with his message.

Ezekiel was called on to embody, to live, God's truth. In our own way we are also called. How do we live the word as deed?

Ezekiel 4:13-15—Questioning God

In these verses, Ezekiel seems to come to the limit of his endurance. His strict training for the priesthood taught him to abhor anything unclean. Eating food cooked on human excrement is evidently more than he can bear.

God senses his distress. God relents and gives him cow dung for fuel. Though God gives Ezekiel a harsh task, God is not unyielding.

When have you taken on a task for God? How did God prepare you for the task? How did God provide for you as you did the job? Has God ever answered your unasked pleas for help?

GENESIS to REVELATION **EZEKIEL**

I am about to bring a sword against you. (6:3)

THE FATE OF JERUSALEM

Ezekiel 6–11

DIMENSION ONE: WHAT DOES THE BIBLE SAY?

Answer these questions by reading Ezekiel 6

1. Why does Ezekiel direct his prophecy toward the mountains of Israel? (6:3-7)

2. Whose idols are to be broken and destroyed? (6:5)

3. Who will escape this particular judgment? (6:8-9)

4. What is God's purpose in the punishment of Israel? (6:10)

Answer these questions by reading Ezekiel 7

5. How is Ezekiel to begin his messages to Israel? (7:2)

THE FATE OF JERUSALEM

6. By what is Israel to be judged? (7:3, 8, 27)

7. What is "the day" spoken of in verse 10? (7:19)

8. What have the people looked to for security that will fail them in the day of the Lord? (7:19, 26-27)

Answer these questions by reading Ezekiel 8

9. What happens to Ezekiel as he sits in his house? (8:1)

10. How is Ezekiel transported to Jerusalem? (8:3)

11. What is driving the Lord from the sanctuary? (8:6)

12. What are these detestable things? (8:10-11, 14-17)

Answer these questions by reading Ezekiel 9

13. Whom does the Lord call to the Temple from the north? (9:1-2)

4. Which people of Jerusalem are to be saved? (9:4)

15. Why is the land full of bloodshed and the city full of injustice? (9:9)

Answer these questions by reading Ezekiel 10

16. How does Ezekiel identify the living creatures from chapter 1? (10:1, 15)

17. What is the man clothed in linen to scatter over Jerusalem? (10:2)

18. What details does Ezekiel add about the appearance of the cherubim and the wheels? (10:8, 14)

Answer these questions by reading Ezekiel 11

19. Why is Ezekiel to prophesy against the men gathered at the entrance to the gate? (11:2)

20. What have the people followed instead of God's laws? (11:12)

21. What concerns Ezekiel about Pelatiah's death? (11:13)

22. What will God do to ensure Israel's survival? (11:17)

23. What will be changed once the exiles return? (11:19-20)

24. What does Ezekiel do when the vision leaves him in Babylonia? (11:25)

THE FATE OF JERUSALEM

DIMENSION TWO: WHAT DOES THE BIBLE MEAN?

■ **Ezekiel 6–7.** Chapters 6 and 7 are announcements of judgment against Israel. Chapters 8–11 describe a vision in which Ezekiel is transported to the Temple in Jerusalem.

The "mountains of Israel," to whom this prophecy is addressed, include all of Israel (Ezekiel 7:2).

A prophecy is a direct word from God through the prophet to the people. This particular prophecy is an announcement of judgment. In general, these announcements have (1) an introduction, or a call to attention; (2) a description of the sins of those addressed; and (3) a proclamation of the consequences of these sins.
Ezekiel 6:1-7. These verses have the following structure as an announcement of judgment: (1) a call to attention (v. 3a), and (2) the description and proclamation combined (vv. 3b-7).

In many cases, the form of announcement speeches varies. But the message of each one is that God's judgment is announced to Israel because of its sins.
■ **Ezekiel 6:2.** God had already warned Israel of the consequences of disobedience (Leviticus 26:14-17). To "set your face against" expresses hostility (Jeremiah 21:10). God's face "shining" on Israel in blessing denotes the opposite (see Numbers 6:22-27).
■ **Ezekiel 6:5-7.** God will be revealed to Israel in the destruction of all that it has built up in sin.
■ **Ezekiel 6:8-10.** Here the message is changed from total judgment (vv. 4-7) to escape for some (vv. 8-10). Perhaps verses 8-10 were placed here by an editor who used a later speech by Ezekiel. This shift expresses some hope to his readers at this point of seeming total destruction (Ezekiel 6:9-10). To "remember" is to lay hold of the truth and to live by it.

The "heart" is Israel's inner being. The "eye" is the bridge between this inner being and the outer world (Numbers 15:39).

- **Ezekiel 6:11-14.** These verses continue Ezekiel's announcement of judgment. They are an expansion of the description and proclamation found in verses 3-7.
- **Ezekiel 6:13.** This verse emphasizes the familiar theme of God's determination that "they will know that I am the LORD." The punishments listed here are the same as those found in verses 4-6.
- **Ezekiel 6:14.** Here we read that "from the desert to Diblah" the people will know that the Lord is God. Diblah ("Riblah" in NRSV) is a city on the Orontes River, just north of the boundary between Israel and Syria. The desert, also called the Negev, is the desert or wilderness in southern Judah.
- **Ezekiel 7:1-4.** In this prophecy, Ezekiel addresses the land of Israel. The prophet announces the end or doom of this land. This end is death and destruction by foreigners. The "most wicked of nations" will come against God's chosen nation (v. 24).
- **Ezekiel 7:5-9.** This second prophecy begins with the formula "This is what the Sovereign LORD says." This formula commonly introduces prophetic speeches in the Old Testament.
- **Ezekiel 7:7.** Ezekiel announces that "the day is near." This day will not be as expected. *The day of the Lord* is a term that once indicated a time when God would intervene on the side of Israel against its enemies. Ezekiel and Amos (Amos 5:18-20) see the day as the end for Israel. At this time, God will punish the people for their sins. This end is death (Genesis 6:13).
- **Ezekiel 7:8-10.** God's judgment will be in accordance with human sin. This idea is similar to the fruit of sin (Romans 7:4-5). That is echoed in the poetry of verses 10-11. The words *budded* and *blossomed* denote fruit.
- **Ezekiel 7:12.** This verse is a kind of poetic refrain that the prophet may have used when delivering this prophecy. Hebrew poetry uses parallelism, in which one line repeats or expands the idea of a preceding line: "The time has come! / The day has arrived! / Let not the buyer rejoice / nor the seller grieve."

THE FATE OF JERUSALEM

- **Ezekiel 7:21, 24.** "The wicked of the earth" and "the most wicked of nations" are the Babylonians.
- **Ezekiel 7:22.** "The place I treasure" is the Temple, or the Holy of Holies within the Temple.
- **Ezekiel 8:1.** This vision comes to Ezekiel on September 17, 592 BC.
- **Ezekiel 8:3.** Ezekiel is said to be transported by the Spirit, in order to receive this vision from God at "the entrance of the north gate of the inner court." This entrance is to the third gate leading north from the palace to the Temple. The "idol that provokes to jealousy" was perhaps found in a niche in one of the walls of the gate.
- **Ezekiel 8:7-13.** The seventy elders are representatives of Israel (Exodus 24:1, 9; Numbers 11:16). They worship the images of creatures that are unacceptable for food, much less for worship (Deuteronomy 4:16-18).
- **Ezekiel 8:16-17.** Here the prophet speaks of twenty-five men who were worshiping the sun toward the east. This passage possibly refers to Egyptian ritual practices related to sun-worship.

  Ezekiel says that these men are "putting the branch to their nose." The prophet may be using an idiom meaning "to harass or irritate, to turn one's nose up" at God.
- **Ezekiel 9:1.** God calls executioners ("those who are appointed to execute judgment") to come into the city, "each with a weapon in his hand." These persons are similar to the avenging angel in 2 Kings 19:35.
- **Ezekiel 9:8-11.** After hearing about the punishment that is to come upon the people of Israel, Ezekiel cries out in despair. He wants to intercede for his fellow Israelites. God responds to Ezekiel's question by telling again of Israel's sins. Here God speaks of murder and injustice instead of corrupt worship. In Ezekiel's thought, social and religious sins result from a lack of right relationship with God.
- **Ezekiel 11:2.** "Plotting evil" and "giving wicked advice" may refer to plots against Nebuchadnezzar by Israelites who were Zedekiah's pro-Egyptian advisers.

■ **Ezekiel 11:3.** The "pot" refers to the city as a cooking pot, with city leaders as the "meat in it." The city leaders feel they are protected when they are in the city. However, God's chosen city offers no protection to sinners. God's presence in the Temple and in Israel's history only highlights their sin.

■ **Ezekiel 11:4-12.** Far from being protected, these men will be brought out of Jerusalem to face the swords of foreigners. The only persons protected in Jerusalem will be those already slain.

■ **Ezekiel 11:14-21.** This announcement of salvation reassures the exiles that God is with them. God is a sanctuary to them apart from any sacred building. Prayer and obedience are to be practiced, even in exile.

In verse 15, those left in Jerusalem express their belief that the exiles suffer as sinners under God's judgment, while they enjoy God's grace in the possession of the homeland.

DIMENSION THREE: WHAT DOES THE BIBLE MEAN TO ME?

Ezekiel 6:1-7, 11-14; 7:1-4, 5-27—Prophetic Announcements of Judgment

In this session, we have spoken about prophetic announcements of judgment. We have emphasized that the form and vocabulary may vary, but all prophetic announcements of judgment reveal the word of God to the people. What is the message that Ezekiel is giving to the exiles through his prophetic announcements of judgment? What is the message that Ezekiel is giving us today?

Ezekiel 8–11—To Stand in Awe

In this section, Ezekiel speaks of both judgment and salvation. In many places in his letters, Paul has this double emphasis as well. Where do you see judgment and salvation evident today? How are these ideas expressed in personal and world events? Is one of God's actions more evident than the other? Why?

Son of man, you are living among a rebellious people. (12:2)

3
FAITHLESSNESS BRINGS EXILE AND DESOLATION
Ezekiel 12–15

DIMENSION ONE: WHAT DOES THE BIBLE SAY?

Answer these questions by reading Ezekiel 12

1. What is Ezekiel commanded to prepare for himself? (12:3)

2. What is he then to do? (12:3-6)

3. Why is Ezekiel to do this? (12:6)

4. How is Ezekiel to explain his actions? (12:9-12)

5. Why are Jerusalem and Israel to be punished? (12:19)

6. What mistake do the people make in interpreting the prophet's messages? (12:27)

Answer these questions by reading Ezekiel 13

7. To whom is Ezekiel directing his prophecies? (13:2)

8. Why is Ezekiel to do this? (13:3, 6)

9. To what are the false prophecies likened? (13:10)

10. What have the false prophetesses done to bring God's punishment? (13:23)

Answer these questions by reading Ezekiel 14

11. What have the elders who inquire about God done? (14:3)

12. What is the Lord's purpose in punishing the people? (14:5, 11)

13. Of what are these idolaters and false prophets guilty? (14:11)

14. What four acts of judgment will the Lord send on Jerusalem? (14:13, 15, 17, 19)

FAITHLESSNESS BRINGS EXILE AND DESOLATION

15. The presence of what three righteous men could not save Israel? (14:14, 20)

16. What are the consequences for Israel since Noah, Daniel, and Job could save only themselves? (14:14, 16, 18, 20)

17. What will console Ezekiel? (14:22-23)

Answer these questions by reading Ezekiel 15

18. To what are the inhabitants of Jerusalem compared? (15:6)

19. What does God say about the usefulness of the wood of the vine? (15:5)

20. What does this allegory imply about the usefulness of the inhabitants of Jerusalem? (15:1-7)

21. What have the people done to make God angry with them? (15:8)

DIMENSION TWO: WHAT DOES THE BIBLE MEAN?

■ **Ezekiel 12:3-5.** Jeremiah tells those in Jerusalem of Israel's fate (Jeremiah 10:17-18). Ezekiel is to demonstrate this to the exiles ("as they watch," vv. 3-4). He is to give no explanation until the next morning (v. 8).

An exile's baggage includes the barest essentials: some food and water, cooking utensils, bedding, and perhaps an extra cloak. Ezekiel is to carry this simple baggage from his home to another place. This other place could not be far away. Ezekiel is back the next morning to deliver a clarifying word from God to the exiles (v. 8).

Ezekiel is to leave in the evening, since any long journey would begin once the heat of the day is over. He can easily break ("dig through") the mud-brick wall of his house. This breaking could symbolize a secret escape, as during a siege. It could also symbolize the destruction caused by the siege. Many houses in Judah at that time had stone foundations and walls of mud-brick.

■ **Ezekiel 12:6-7.** Covering the face denotes shame (Genesis 38:15) and suffering (2 Samuel 15:30). It also hides the lost homeland from the exile on his journey.

■ **Ezekiel 12:17-20.** Ezekiel is again to take on the bodily suffering of his people as a witness to God's judgment (see Ezekiel 4). The necessary events of eating and drinking will be done in fear and trembling because he realizes the coming devastation. Ezekiel's fear and trembling in the face of God's truth are in contrast to the false security of those living in sin.

The phrase in verse 19, "the people of the land," refers to the exiles. The phrase may also mean the common people (Ezekiel 7:27). It could also mean the body of free landowners in a certain area who hold political and military power. That the politically powerless exiles are addressed in this way is ironic.

■ **Ezekiel 12:26-28.** Here God is arguing against a saying that is common in the language of the people. This proverb places the judgment upon the people way in the future. But, God's word has already begun to act. When Ezekiel, or any other prophet, is called to prophesy, the fulfillment of God's word begins. Evading God's word is impossible.

False prophecy could have been a considerable obstacle to Ezekiel's preaching, as it was for Jeremiah (Jeremiah 23:9-32; 29:8, 15, 21-23). Through Ezekiel, God condemns the perversion of God's word by false prophets wherever they appear.

FAITHLESSNESS BRINGS EXILE AND DESOLATION

■ **Ezekiel 13:3.** Ezekiel 13 speaks of the problems of false prophecy and idolatry. Ezekiel argues against the messages of false prophets and the methods they use to receive their messages. He accuses the false prophets of following their own spirits instead of God. A true prophet must wait for a word from God (Ezekiel 3:26-27; Jeremiah 23:16-18).

■ **Ezekiel 13:4-5.** Verse 4 is addressed to Israel about these false prophets. The metaphor of the prophets as "jackals among ruins" relates to the devastation of Judah and to the circumstances of the exiles. Jackals, in their natural habitat, can make a home among the ruins of a city. This illustrates that the false prophets are "at home" in Israel's disaster and exploiting it for their own benefit.

The "wall . . . for the house of Israel" is a symbol for the people's spiritual defenses. The false prophets have done nothing to repair the damage done to the covenant community. They have neglected their responsibilities to proclaim and witness to the truth.

■ **Ezekiel 13:11-16.** The physical phenomenon of the coming of the Lord (vv. 11, 13) will overpower the people's false defenses. The false prophets have only whitewashed the walls, not repaired them. When the walls crumble, the people will ask the false prophets why the whitewash did no good (v. 12). The word for wall used in verses 12-15 is normally used for the walls of houses. The outer walls of houses in Judah were sometimes made of stone bonded with mortar. The interior walls were made without mortar.

■ **Ezekiel 14:1-11.** As in Ezekiel 8:1, representatives of the exiles come to inquire of God through Ezekiel. The Bible does not tell us what the questions are. But we can guess they had something to do with the future of Judah or of the exiles.

■ **Ezekiel 14:3.** Ezekiel tells us that the elders look to God as well as to the gods of Babylon. "Have set up idols in their hearts" means that they let their idols become the center of their lives. The heart and eyes are the doors for temptation (see Genesis 3:6; Matthew 6:22-24).

■ **Ezekiel 14:4-5.** God will "recapture" the hearts of those who come to the Lord as parents lay hold of a rebellious child (Deuteronomy 21:18-19). Thus, God will lay hold of all Israel.

■ **Ezekiel 14:6-8.** God's judgment of sin is a call to repentance. This call invites those who accept it to be saved. Verse 6 states what the people must do to repent and return their hearts to God.

■ **Ezekiel 14:9-11.** Here again we see language that is legal in nature (see also Ezekiel 3:19). These verses expand the prophecy in verses 4-8. In the present passage, we read about prophets who are deceived into giving guidance to idolaters. Verse 9 echoes the conviction of Deuteronomy 13:1-5, that God may test the people through false prophets.

Those who seek God's help must surrender to God's will (Jeremiah 38:14-28).

■ **Ezekiel 14:12-23.** This section of chapter 14 is divided into two parts (vv. 12-20, 21-23). The first part covers the issues of individual responsibility and of God's power over all countries and peoples. The second part deals especially with Jerusalem, its coming punishment, and the consolation to come after the punishment.

Noah, Daniel, and Job are mentioned as exemplary people who could still save only themselves by their righteousness (see vv. 14, 16, 18, 20). Israel may not rely on the righteous ones of the past. Obedience must be ongoing. Even Noah, who did save his family (Genesis 7–9), could not save them now (Ezekiel 14:18).

■ **Ezekiel 14:21-23.** The general judgment on "a land" is made specific here and applied to the city of Jerusalem. The survivors from Jerusalem will display unrighteous and faithless behavior among the exiles ("they will come to you"). By this behavior they will show the righteousness of God's punishment upon Jerusalem. This punishment will be a consolation in itself. The punishment will show God's unfailing judgment and also God's unfailing covenant promise.

■ **Ezekiel 15.** In chapter 15, Ezekiel tells his fellow exiles about the fate of Jerusalem. This parable probably dates from sometime before 587 BC. The lesson taught by the parable of the vine (Ezekiel 15:2-5) is not a general truth. Rather, it is an announcement of punishment (Ezekiel 15:6-8). Teaching through parables is used by teachers of wisdom (1 Kings

FAITHLESSNESS BRINGS EXILE AND DESOLATION

4:29-34), by the prophets (2 Samuel 12:1-6; Amos 5:19), and by God (Jeremiah 18).

■ **Ezekiel 15:2.** The "wood of a vine" in this verse is used as a metaphor for Israel. The metaphor of Israel as a vine has been used many places in the Bible (see Psalm 80; Isaiah 5:1-7; Jeremiah 2:21; Hosea 10:1).

DIMENSION THREE: WHAT DOES THE BIBLE MEAN TO ME?

Ezekiel 13:1-16—False Prophecy

This portion of Scripture concentrates on the idea of false prophecy. This is a common issue in Ezekiel, as in many of the Old Testament prophets. Prophets and people alike in ancient times were concerned about recognizing false prophecy for what it is.

In Ezekiel 13:1-16, we have two instructions for discerning God's true word. First, we must decide if the prophetic word points to God for authentication. Second, we must lead lives of holiness and godliness. We must also have a right relationship with God.

Are these instructions sufficient for discerning true prophecy from false prophecy? How can we use Scripture as a standard to measure a so-called word from God?

Ezekiel 14:6-8—The Prophet and Idolatry

In Ezekiel 12–15 the main concern of the prophet is what results from faithlessness to God and unrighteous living. Consequences of such behavior include coming under the influence of false prophecy and idolatry.

What practices do you associate idolatry with today? Why is it especially important for prophets to avoid associating with idols and idolaters? Are there other persons, then and now, who should have similar restrictions? Who are these persons? Why and how should they be restricted?

*Repent! Turn away from all your offenses;
then sin will not be your downfall. (18:30)*

FROM GOD'S SAVING ACTS TO GRIEF

Ezekiel 16–19

DIMENSION ONE: WHAT DOES THE BIBLE SAY?

Answer these questions by reading Ezekiel 16

1. As Ezekiel reviews the events of Jerusalem's past, what are the people to be reminded of? (16:3-14)

2. How does God describe Jerusalem? (16:4, 7)

3. How is the special relationship between God and Jerusalem described? (16:8)

4. To what does God compare unfaithful Jerusalem? (16:15)

5. How does Jerusalem use God's gifts (16:16-21)

FROM GOD'S SAVING ACTS TO GRIEF

6. What did Jerusalem forget? (16:22, 43)

7. Who will God use to destroy the prostitute? (16:37-41)

8. What will God then remember and do? (16:60)

Answer these questions by reading Ezekiel 17

9. How is Ezekiel to deliver God's words to Israel? (17:2)

10. Does Israel understand the parable? (17:12)

11. What phrase indicates that God will stand by these words? (17:16, 19)

12. How will God ensure Israel's survival? (17:22-23)

13. What unexpected things does God do? (17:24)

Answer these questions by reading Ezekiel 18

14. What is the point of the proverb in 18:2? (18:19)

15. What lesson does the story in verses 1-24 teach? (18:4, 20, 24)

16. What does Israel say against God? (18:29)

17. What is Israel's hope? (18:30-31)

18. Why does God offer Israel a chance to "repent and live"? (18:32)

Answer these questions by reading Ezekiel 19

19. How is chapter 19 different from chapters 16–18? (19:1-14)

20. What type of poetry is chapter 19? (19:1)

21. For whom does Ezekiel lament? (19:1)

22. How are the princes and their mother described? (19:2-3, 5, 10-11)

23. What happens to the princely young lions? (19:4, 9)

24. What happens to the vine? (19:13-14)

DIMENSION TWO: WHAT DOES THE BIBLE MEAN?

■ **Ezekiel 16.** There are three blocks of material within chapter 16: verses 1-43a, the allegory of the abandoned child; verses 43b-58, the allegory of the three sisters; and verses 59-63, a promise of covenant renewal. Each of these blocks speaks of God's relationship to Jerusalem as a child or wife. The allegorical form is used to accuse Jerusalem and to make plain the judgment that comes from sin (also see Ezekiel 17; 19; 23; 31; 34).

- **Ezekiel 16:1-43a.** Verses 1-34 declare the history of God's relationship to Jerusalem and its scorn of God's care. Verses 35-43a announce the judgment that follows Jerusalem's sin. In this sense, Jerusalem represents all Israel.
- **Ezekiel 16:1-3a.** Ezekiel opens his message to Jerusalem with the familiar prophetic phrase, "This is what the Sovereign LORD says."
- **Ezekiel 16:3b-14.** The story of a foundling child, saved and raised by a benefactor, was a common folktale of Ezekiel's time. Here, such a tale is used to tell that Jerusalem's life and well-being are the result of God's care.
- **Ezekiel 16:9-14.** The washing and anointing may reflect the ritual preparation for a marriage ceremony. The nose ring probably comes from Bedouin customs. The crown is a bridal adornment.
- **Ezekiel 16:15-34.** This section tells of the abuse of God's gifts by the bride and of the punishment that follows. Part of the material here may be a later elaboration by Ezekiel or one of his disciples on the basic content of verses 15, 24-25. This elaboration could be based on the content and vocabulary of Ezekiel 23.
- **Ezekiel 16:16-21.** The prostitutions of Jerusalem are both literal and figurative. The people practice cult prostitution similar to Canaanite nature worship, and they are unfaithful to their true god. Nature worship and religious prostitution were common in the time of Manasseh (687–642 BC, 2 Kings 21:1-18) and of Zedekiah (597–587 BC, Ezekiel 8).
- **Ezekiel 16:35-43a.** Judgment is announced. Verse 36 tells why, reflecting verses 15-20. Verse 37 begins the list of the consequences of what has gone before.
- **Ezekiel 16:43b-58.** The theme of Jerusalem's pagan lineage is picked up from verse 3 and elaborated. Sodom

and Samaria were neighbors of Jerusalem and Judah whose past sins are well known (see Genesis 19:4-5, 24-25; Isaiah 1:9). Being compared to these corrupt cities is a hard blow for Jerusalem.

- **Ezekiel 17.** In chapter 17, Ezekiel is told to ask Israel a riddle in the form of an allegory. Verses 3-10 and 22-24 are written in metrical form. In Hebrew, this form usually has lines of six stresses that are divided into half-lines of three stresses each. Verses 11-21, which provide an interpretation of the riddle, are more in prose form.
- **Ezekiel 18.** In chapter 18, God gives Ezekiel a prophecy that disputes another common proverb (Ezekiel 12:21-28). This prophecy teaches the exiles that an individual is responsible for his or her own sin and its consequences (Ezekiel 14:12-22).
- **Ezekiel 18:5-18.** This section uses the example of three generations of men to confirm and illustrate the principle laid down in verse 4. Its style is legalistic, similar to that of the Holiness Code in Leviticus 17–26. As a priest, Ezekiel would know these laws and those of Deuteronomy quite well.
- **Ezekiel 19.** Verse 1 identifies the poetry of chapter 19 as a death lament. Poetic laments were originally used in rites for the dead in Israel (see 2 Samuel 3:31-34). Laments were also used in worship by individuals and the congregation when they were in supplication before God. They bewailed misfortune and asked for help (Psalms 51; 129).

The laments of Isaiah 14 and of the Book of Lamentations follow in this same line. These passages lament political events that had already happened. Isaiah 14 also combines elements of the lament and the mocking song that tell of God's victory over enemies. In Amos 5:1-3 a lament for the "Fallen . . . Virgin Israel" is a prophetic announcement of judgment pointing to the future.

- **Ezekiel 19:2.** The "lions" are the princes of Judah. Depending upon the identity given to the lion whelps, the mother may be the Davidic dynasty or specifically

Hamultal, the wife of Josiah and the mother of Jehoahaz and Zedekiah. Genesis 49:9 uses the metaphor of Judah as a lion's whelp. The royal lion is also found on Israelite seals and on Solomon's throne (see 1 Kings 10:18-20).

■ **Ezekiel 19:12-14.** The "east wind" is Babylon. The fruit stripped from the vine (v. 12) and the absence of a strong stem for a "ruler's scepter" (v. 14) suggest the execution of Zedekiah's sons at Riblah (2 Kings 25:6-7; Jeremiah 52:9-11). Zedekiah was taken in exile to Babylon. In this way, he was transplanted in a "dry and thirsty land" (v. 13).

DIMENSION THREE: WHAT DOES THE BIBLE MEAN TO ME?

What Can Prophetic Speech Teach Us?

This lesson contains examples of different kinds of prophetic speech. Each speech form spoke to Ezekiel's audience in a unique way. In addition, each kind of prophetic speech has a special message for readers of the Scripture today.

How does the form of a message from or about God affect our understanding of it? How does form influence our understanding of any message?

Does narrative speak more clearly than allegory or poetry? Do allegory and poetry and metaphorical narratives require more thought and consideration on our part? How are they effective in claiming our attention? Do poetry and metaphor speak to us on an emotional as well as rational level? What value does this quality have? In what way does appeal to our emotions hinder us in expressing our faith?

Think about your favorite passages from the Bible. Are they narrative, poetry, allegory, parable, legal discourse? What is special about them? What do they teach you?

Son of man, set your face against Jerusalem and preach against the sanctuary. (21:2)

A HISTORY OF SIN AND ITS CONSEQUENCES

Ezekiel 20–24

DIMENSION ONE: WHAT DOES THE BIBLE SAY?

Answer these questions by reading Ezekiel 20

1. When do the elders of Israel come to Ezekiel to inquire of the Lord? (20: I)

2. Does the text say what they want from God? (20:1-3)

3. Of what historical events does God remind the elders? (20:6, 10, 28)

4. In each situation, how do the Israelites behave? (20:8, 16, 27, 30)

5. Why does God withhold anger and wrath? (20:9, 22)

A HISTORY OF SIN AND ITS CONSEQUENCES

6. Why will God not allow the elders in exile to inquire of God? (20:30-32)

7. When will Israel know God and mend its ways? (20:42)

8. What shall devour the south? (20:47)

9. What do Ezekiel's listeners say about him? (20:49)

Answer these questions by reading Ezekiel 21

10. What is Ezekiel to preach and prophesy? (21:3)

11. Whose sword does the Lord send against Israel? (21:19)

12. Against what other nation will the Lord's sword be drawn? (21:28) Why? (21:29)

Answer these questions by reading Ezekiel 22

13. What sins does the Lord cite against Israel? (22:6-12)

14. Which groups in Israel are named in God's indictment? (22:25-29)

Answer these questions by reading Ezekiel 23

15. Which countries do the prostitute sisters Oholah and Oholibah represent? (23:4)

16. With whom do Oholah and Oholibah engage in prostitution? (23:5, 12, 17)

17. Whom does God use to punish the prostitutes? (23:9, 22-23)

18. What are the consequences for Oholah and Oholibah? (23:49)

Answer these questions by reading Ezekiel 24

19. When does Ezekiel receive the next prophecy? (24:1)

20. What happens on that day? (24:2)

21. What is "the pot" about to be boiled and cleansed? (24:6)

22. Why is Ezekiel not to outwardly mourn his wife's death? (24:16-17, 24)

23. What is the great loss? (24:21)

A HISTORY OF SIN AND ITS CONSEQUENCES

24. What will Israel do instead of mourn? (24:23)

25. How will Ezekiel be changed after he receives the news of Jerusalem's fall? (24:27)

DIMENSION TWO: WHAT DOES THE BIBLE MEAN?

Background. With this lesson we come to the close of the first large section in the Book of Ezekiel. (The other sections are chs. 25–32; 33–48). Chapters 20–23 tell the history of Israel's sins and of the consequences. They tell of Israel's disobedience, wickedness, and death. Chapter 24 announces the end of Jerusalem's opportunities for rebellion and reveals the strength of Ezekiel's commitment to his call.

■ **Ezekiel 20:1.** On August 14, 591 BC, elders of the exiles went to question God through Ezekiel (14:1-11; 8:1). This was in the seventh year of Jehoiachin's exile.

■ **Ezekiel 20:2-4.** As in Ezekiel 14:3-4, 7-8, God answers the inquirers in a way they probably do not expect. Their questions, which are not stated, are to be answered indirectly in God's own way. In God's question to Ezekiel in verse 4a, God gives a clear indication that judgment is to be announced to the elders. Verse 4b introduces the direction and form this judgment will take. The reasons for judgment will begin with a history of Israel's faith (see Deuteronomy 26:5-11; Exodus 13:8).

■ **Ezekiel 20:10-14.** The next saving act in Israel's history was the giving of the law in the desert (v. 11). The law is divided into statutes and ordinances, and sacred and civil regulations. The observance of these laws gives life (see also Leviticus 18:5). Yet, Israel rejects these saving acts and invites God's wrath (v. 13). God remains true to the plan for salvation and deliverance (v. 14).

■ **Ezekiel 20:15-17.** God does not make a full end of Israel, but that rebellious generation in the wilderness will not possess the Promised Land.

■ **Ezekiel 20:18-22.** The children of the Exodus generation will have a reprieve. They will have a chance to be faithful participants in the covenant. In Exodus 31:17, the sabbath is a sign. It reminds the Israelites that God rested on the seventh day. Ezekiel 20:20 adds the recognition of the sabbath as a sign that the people know "that I am the LORD your God" (also see Exodus 19:4-6; Deuteronomy 14:2).

■ **Ezekiel 20:27-29.** These verses could have been added by a later editor, who perhaps wished to add a note on Israel's history of sin in the Promised Land. Another possibility is that verse 28 (also v. 29) has been misplaced. In that case, it should follow verse 22. Then God's withholding wrath would be followed by another chance for life, as in verses 10 and 18.

Also, the word *them* in verse 28 should logically be the children of verse 18-21 instead of the fathers (*them* of v. 15). The fathers of the desert generation were denied access to the Promised Land (Ezekiel 20:15; Numbers 14:20-23). It would then be their children who are given the land, only to fall into sin themselves (v. 28).

■ **Ezekiel 20:37-38.** Verse 37 alludes to the practice of a shepherd who has each animal in his flock walk under his outstretched staff so that he may count them and separate those he does not want to keep (Jeremiah 33:13; Leviticus 27:32). The fate of the purged rebels is exclusion from the land of Israel. The purging prepares Israel for a new age of obedience and knowledge of God. Once again, Ezekiel presents a decisive contrast between the human capacity for willful disobedience and sin and the ever-present power and will of the Lord to have the people as God's own.

■ **Ezekiel 20:39.** Total devotion to idols is preferable to divided loyalties that profane the holy name of God.

■ **Ezekiel 20:40-44.** True and uncompromised worship of God will take place only where God chooses. Zion ("my

A HISTORY OF SIN AND ITS CONSEQUENCES

holy mountain") will be restored (chs. 40–48) and the people brought back in purity. This will be evident even to the world at large. There will be no doubt as to God's holiness and power. God deals with the people in love, whether in judgment or salvation.

■ **Ezekiel 20:45-49.** In the Hebrew Bible, verse 45 is Ezekiel 21:1. Chapter 21 then would have thirty-seven verses. Verses 45-48 are an allegorical prophecy of judgment against the south. This prophecy is interpreted in Ezekiel 21:1-5. The word *south* should be used (as it is in the NIV) throughout verse 46 and verse 47 instead of *Negeb* (as in the NRSV). The term *south* indicates a general area, not a particular geographical location.

The structure of verse 46 is paralleled in 21:2. Verse 48 is paralleled in 21:5. The metaphor of fire consuming the vine (15:4-7) and the ruler's scepter (19:12, 14) is similar to this fire, which will consume the forest, Israel. That all flesh will recognize the divine origin of the fire shows that Israel's punishment will be seen by the whole world.

In verse 49, Ezekiel indirectly asks God for an interpretation of the word God has spoken. Ezekiel mediates for the exiles, who might ignore his message as mere stories.

■ **Ezekiel 21:21-23.** Nebuchadnezzar uses divination to decide which way he will strike at the rebels. He puts marked arrows into a bag, or quiver, and then draws one out at random. The markings on the drawn arrow indicate what was to happen. He consults small idols representing household gods, known as *teraphim*, though their exact use in divination is unknown (Genesis 31:19; Hosea 3:4). Nebuchadnezzar also examines the liver of a sheep for signs. The Babylonians were well known for this type of divination. They considered the liver to be the source of blood and thus of life itself. Specially trained priests examined the liver of the sacrificial sheep. Clay models of the liver were made with inscriptions to guide the diviners.

GENESIS to REVELATION EZEKIEL

- **Ezekiel 21:23.** Once the decisive lot falls on Jerusalem, the elements of the coming siege are named.
- **Ezekiel 21:24.** The people of Jerusalem dispute the outcome of Nebuchadnezzar's divination. The solemn oaths they swore (Ezekiel 17:13, 19) apparently mean nothing. Thus, Nebuchadnezzar is to prove their guilt.
- **Ezekiel 22:13-16.** In verses 13 and 14, the Lord claps (Ezekiel 21:17) and begins to deal out Jerusalem's punishment. As in Ezekiel 17:24, God assures the people that the divine word shall be accomplished.

    Verses 15-16 may be a later addition that shows how the judgment will be fulfilled. God allows the holy name to be shamed through Israel's downfall. This will convince Israel of how its wickedness was already shaming God.
- **Ezekiel 22:17-22.** The fierce words of punishment in this prophecy have a strong visual and emotional impact. The smelting that takes place is not intended to separate precious metal from dross (Isaiah 1:25). All of Israel is dross to be gathered into the furnace of Jerusalem to be melted in an outpouring of the wrath of God.
- **Ezekiel 23:14.** The sisters begin their prostitution in Egypt, even before they are chosen by God. The descriptions of their behavior are explicit and coarse (see vv. 3, 8, 17, 20). As in chapter 16, the covenant relationship is once again spoken of as a marriage.
- **Ezekiel 23:5-10.** The political dealings of Israel with Assyria, and with Egypt in trying to throw off Assyrian domination, led to involvement in foreign cults (see 2 Kings 15:19-29; 17:1-14 for more information about the alliances). Because of her disloyalty to the covenant and to her marriage vows, God delivers Oholah to her former lovers, the Assyrians (see Ezekiel 16:35-43).
- **Ezekiel 23:14-17.** Ezekiel's description of the wall frescoes fits those used in Babylon. The Chaldeans were Arameans who originally lived beside the Persian Gulf. They took over Babylon in 625 BC, and took the Assyrian capital of Nineveh in 612 BC. By 605 BC, Judah was taken into the

Babylonian sphere. At first, Judah courts the favor of the rising Babylonian power (Ezekiel 16:28-29; 23:17a); then later turns away in disgust (v. 17b) after finding no special position within the empire.

- **Ezekiel 23:18.** Oholibah's husband (God) "turned away from her" because of her prostitution.
- **Ezekiel 23:19-21.** Failure to win favor from Babylon brings on more political intrigue with Egypt.
- **Ezekiel 23:40-44.** This passage might be an account of a heathen feast. It could possibly be a marginal note in a manuscript that was incorporated into the text.
- **Ezekiel 23:45-49.** These verses sum up history and its consequences. All nations ("all women") should take this as a lesson and recognize the authority of almighty God who brings judgment on an unfaithful family.
- **Ezekiel 24:16-17.** God prepares Ezekiel for the death of his wife. God tells him how he must react to this severe loss. Ezekiel can take comfort only in knowing that he is in alliance with God. His life is bound up in God's purpose of reaching God's wayward people. Ezekiel is to raise no loud lament for his dead loved one. He is not, against custom, to go bareheaded and barefoot, to wear sackcloth, or to attend a funeral feast after a time of fasting.
- **Ezekiel 24:18-24.** Ezekiel explains his actions to the exiles. Jerusalem will be destroyed (v. 21). The exiles' only reaction will be grief so deep and numbing that they will give no outward sign of it except groaning (vv. 22-23). Here the words of God (vv. 21, 24) and those of Ezekiel (vv. 22-23) are mingled with no transition between the two. As a sign of God (v. 24), Ezekiel proclaims God's word and is also part of the process that sets its accomplishment in motion. The exiles will no longer be able to avoid the truth that God is in their midst (v. 24c).

DIMENSION THREE: WHAT DOES THE BIBLE MEAN TO ME?

Ezekiel, Psalm 106, and History

As we read Ezekiel and Psalms, we are reading our own history. Israel's history is our history because we are in the same line of faith. The highs and lows of Israel's relationship to God are symbolic of similar experiences in our own relationship to God.

How do our failures and successes of the past have value other than merely in our remembering them? What particular failures in our personal, national, or church history give grounds for calling on the Lord in hope? If we were to write our own Psalm 106, what would it say?

In Romans 9:25-26, Paul quotes Hosea 2:23 to offer assurance that God works to claim the people, even in their sin. In Romans 8:38-39, Paul assures us that nothing in all creation will separate us from the love of God. Does "nothing" include our own past sins? Why or why not?

They will live in safety when I inflict punishment on all their neighbors who maligned them. (28:26)

PROPHECIES AGAINST THE NATIONS

Ezekiel 25–28

DIMENSION ONE: WHAT DOES THE BIBLE SAY?

Answer these questions by reading Ezekiel 25

1. Against whom is Ezekiel told to prophesy? (25:2)

2. Why is God handing the Ammonites over to their enemies? (25:3, 6)

3. Against what other nations will God execute judgment? (25:8, 12, 15)

4. What will these nations learn from their punishment? (25:11, 17)

GENESIS to REVELATION EZEKIEL

Answer these questions by reading Ezekiel 26

5. When did the prophecy against Tyre come to Ezekiel? (26:1)

6. Why will Tyre be punished? (26:2)

7. How will the Lord destroy Tyre? (26:7)

8. Who will raise a lament over Tyre? (26:16-17)

Answer these questions by reading Ezekiel 27

9. After the prophecy of doom, how is Ezekiel to speak of Tyre? (27:2)

10. How is Tyre described in the lament? (27:3-9)

11. What was Tyre before its fall? (27:33)

12. What is its fate? (27:36)

Answer these questions by reading Ezekiel 28

13. Why must Ezekiel prophesy against the ruler of Tyre? (28:2)

PROPHECIES AGAINST THE NATIONS

14. Over whom is Ezekiel to lament? (28:12)

15. How is the king's dwelling described? (28:13)

16. Why is the king cast out of Eden? (28:16-18)

17. Against whom must Ezekiel now prophesy? (28:21)

18. What does the destruction of its neighbors mean for Israel? (28:24-26)

DIMENSION TWO: WHAT DOES THE BIBLE MEAN?

■ **Background.** Chapters 25–32 stand apart from the material that comes before and after them. They contain prophecies delivered by Ezekiel to nations other than Israel. These prophecies proclaim God's judgment on the nations. Seven nations are named (Ammon, Moab, Edom, Philistia, Tyre, Sidon, and Egypt) in prophecies and laments of varying lengths.

■ **Ezekiel 25:1-4.** Ezekiel is to address the Ammonites with a word from God. God is judging them because they were jubilant when the Temple was destroyed and the Judeans were taken into exile (v. 3). Ammon will be punished by being made subjects to the "people of the East" (v. 4). These people will execute God's judgment. They are nomadic tribes that come from the desert and steppe region east of the cultivated areas along the eastern side of the Jordan River. Such tribes would plunder settled areas and pasture their flocks in ruined, overgrown cities.

■ **Ezekiel 25:6-7.** This elaboration of the judgment against Ammon may come from one of Ezekiel's disciples. It extends the judgment to total destruction. Perhaps this passage was added to show that Ammon will fare no better than Israel does after showing contempt toward God.

The accusations against Ammon focus on its attitude toward Israel's fate. It is malicious in its joy that the Temple is gone and that God's chosen people are scattered (see Zephaniah 2:8). No mention is made of political shortcomings. Ammon had a long history of political struggles with Israel. God will force Ammon to recognize the Lord's power over all nations. The fate of God's chosen city and people does not change the fact that God is Lord of all.

■ **Ezekiel 25:12-14.** Edom and Israel also had a long history of bitterness and warfare (1 Kings 11:14-22; 2 Kings 14:7). This warfare occurred even though the two were supposed to be descended from brothers (Deuteronomy 23:7-8). Israel was resentful of Edom's occupation of southern Judah (Ezekiel 16:57). The occupation was brought on by pressure on Edom by the people of the East.

Israel, rather than Nebuchadnezzar or the peoples of the East, will be God's instrument of punishment against Edom. Edom will gain knowledge of God's terrible wrath and vengeance.

■ **Ezekiel 26:1-6.** The twelfth year (v. 1) could perhaps be the eleventh year. The form here for the number eleven is not the one usually found in Ezekiel (as in 30:20; 31:1). An early Greek translation reads "the twelfth year." This would be the twelfth year of Jehoiachin (early 586 BC).

Tyre is accused of rejoicing over Jerusalem's fall and of taking material gains from Jerusalem's devastation. The "gate to the nations" swinging open to Tyre may point to its better position on the trade routes from Egypt and Arabia. It may also mean that Tyre sees a long-standing political as well as commercial rival out of the way.

The protection offered Tyre by the sea is turned against it. God brings many nations against it, "like the sea casting up its waves." Tyre, the rock, will be stripped bare and of no use to anyone except the fishermen who spread their nets there to dry.

PROPHECIES AGAINST THE NATIONS

The continuation of the prophecy in verses 5b-6 after the concluding phrase "I have spoken, declares the Sovereign LORD" may be an editorial addition. It brings Tyre's mainland suburbs into the punishment. The coast has shifted between Tyre and the surrounding area since the time of Alexander the Great. Today Tyre is part of the coastland.

■ **Ezekiel 26:19-21.** In verse 19, the ocean depths and its vast waters are the primordial deep on which God had set limits (Genesis 1:2-6). God broke these waters loose at the Flood (Genesis 7:11). These waters are like a subterranean ocean associated with the "depths of the earth" (Psalm 63:9). These depths are the pit (Ezekiel 31:14) or Sheol. Both the pit and the deep are associated with the powers of death.

"The people of long ago" are like "those long dead" (Lamentations 3:6). They live in a dusty, arid world without peace or joy. They illustrate that human pride and earthly power are overwhelmed by the powers of death. The waters of the deep can and do reach into the world of the living to carry them away so that they "will be no more" (v. 21).

■ **Ezekiel 27:3-9.** Tyre is a seafaring, trading city. It has two harbors well suited to accommodate international trade. So Tyre is pictured as a magnificent merchant ship that inspires pride and brings riches and power to the owners. Tyre is addressed directly as the ship, built of the finest material from many lands and manned by a skilled crew.

Tyre is accused of vanity and false pride (v. 3). The city is beautiful and prosperous, but no match for God and the "east wind" (v. 26).

"Senir" (v. 5) is the Amorite name for Mount Hermon (Deuteronomy 3:9). "Bashan" (v. 6) is east of the Sea of Galilee. "Elishah" (v. 7) is possibly Cyprus.

"Blue" (v. 7) is blue-purple, and "purple" is red-purple. The color purple is associated with luxury and splendor (Song of Songs 3:10; Esther 8:15). The purple dye comes from the murex, a sea snail, and is a famous Phoenician export. Murex shells were gathered either by hand in shallow water or in nets from deeper water. It took approximately

12,000 snails to make 114 grams of dye. Chemists have been trying to recreate this dye-making process since the nineteenth century, but without much success.

During the reign of Nabonidus (the last king of Babylon, 555–539 BC), purple wool was forty times more expensive than wool of other colors. In 200 BC, one gram of the precious dye cost eighty-four dollars. That means that one pound would have cost more than $36,660 in today's dollars. Obviously only the very rich could afford garments of this color.

The blue specified in Numbers 15:37-41 is the blue-purple from the murex. The poor could afford perhaps only four blue threads to meet this requirement. *Phoenicia* comes from a Greek word meaning "purple." *Canaan* also means "land of purple."

■ **Ezekiel 27:13.** "Greece" ("Javan" in the NRSV) refers to the Ionian Greeks. Joel 3:4-6 tells of Tyre and Sidon selling the people of Judah to the Greeks as slaves.

Tubal and Meshek are nations on the east and west sides of the Ante-Taurus mountain range in Cappadocia (Ezekiel 38:2). Their chief products are iron and bronze.

■ **Ezekiel 27:29-31.** The reaction of Tyre's seafaring neighbors to its downfall is described at length. They leave their labors to mourn and demonstrate their grief at Tyre's passing. Their actions of distress and mournful wailings are part of the mourning ritual.

■ **Ezekiel 28:3.** The wise Daniel mentioned here is probably the same wise judge named in Ezekiel 14:14-20.

■ **Ezekiel 28:4-5.** The prince's wisdom has brought him and his kingdom great wealth and power (ch. 27), as well as led to false pride (27:3). It also has led to a false sense of security placed in earthly power.

■ **Ezekiel 28:6.** Injustice (Ezekiel 26:2-3) does not bring punishment. They are punished because they lay claim to wisdom and authority that belong to God.

■ **Ezekiel 28:20-23.** This prophetic announcement of judgment against Sidon contains no specific charges against it (see Ezekiel 25:3, 8, 12, 15). The intention of this punishment is to manifest the glory and holiness of God and to impart knowledge of God. Such intentions agree with priestly accounts (Exodus 14:17-18; Leviticus 10:1-3) of manifestations of God as judge of the world. This judgment against Sidon brings to six the number of Israel's neighbors facing punishment from God.

■ **Ezekiel 28:24.** God has warned Israel before of the "briers and sharp thorns (Numbers 33:55; Joshua 23:13).

After proclaiming the fate of Israel's contemptuous neighbors, Ezekiel declares Israel's freedom for them. Even the heathen will be forced to recognize the power of God. Once this is accomplished, God moves on. In their salvation as well as in their punishment (Ezekiel 23:49) the people of Israel "will know that I am the Sovereign LORD."

DIMENSION THREE: WHAT DOES THE BIBLE MEAN TO ME?

God's Power and the Frailty of Human Achievement

Throughout these four chapters, two themes occur again and again. These themes are the universality of God's power and the frailty of human achievement in the face of God's will and power.

How do we respond to these prophecies from Ezekiel? Do we need to respond, or is it enough just to know this part of the history of our faith? One possible response is to examine ourselves in light of the charges brought against Israel and the nations. Are we guilty of violence or, at the very least, bad temper? Are we guilty of greed? False pride? Being self-serving?

Though our sins may not manifest in the same way as those of our ancient brothers and sisters, we sometimes attempt to deny or ignore God's will. What examples of such avoidance or ignorance can you cite?

Read Philippians 2:13. How do we make ourselves more responsive to God, to work God's "good purpose" in us?

Son of man, set your face against Pharaoh king of Egypt and prophesy against him and against all Egypt. (29:2)

7

PROPHECIES AGAINST EGYPT

Ezekiel 29–32

DIMENSION ONE: WHAT DOES THE BIBLE SAY?

Answer these questions by reading Ezekiel 29

1. When does this prophecy come to Ezekiel? (29:1)

2. Against whom does he prophesy? (29:2)

3. What literary form does Ezekiel use to tell Pharaoh of his fate? (29:3-5)

4. Why is Egypt to be punished? (29:6-8, 16)

5. What will happen to Egypt after forty years? (29:13-15)

6. When does God tell Ezekiel that Egypt will be defeated by Nebuchadnezzar's army? (29:17, 19)

PROPHECIES AGAINST EGYPT

Answer these questions by reading Ezekiel 30

7. What will the day of the Lord bring? (30:3)

8. Who will fall along with Egypt? (30:5)

9. Who will be God's instrument for this destruction? (30:10)

10. Why is God doing this to Egypt? (30:19, 26)

11. What does God say is going to happen to Pharaoh? (30:21-22)

Answer these questions by reading Ezekiel 31

12. When does this prophecy to Egypt come to Ezekiel? (31:1-2a)

13. To what does God compare Egypt? (31:2b-3)

14. What other trees does it surpass in size and beauty? (31:8-9)

15. Why will this great tree be cut down? (31:10-11)

16. Who will cut down the tree? (31:12)

17. Where will the tree go after its death? (31:15)

18. What will be its fate in there? (31:18)

Answer these questions by reading Ezekiel 32

19. When does Ezekiel lament over Pharaoh? (32:1)

20. How does God describe Pharaoh? (32:2b)

21. What will the swords of mighty men bring to Egypt? (32:12)

22. What does Ezekiel do on the fifteenth day of the month in the twelfth year? (32:17-18)

23. Whom will Egypt find in "the pit"? (32:22, 24, 26, 29, 30)

24. Why are the slain of these nations in "the depths of the pit" among the uncircumcised? (32:23-24, 26, 30, 32)

DIMENSION TWO: WHAT DOES THE BIBLE MEAN?

■ **Ezekiel 29.** Chapter 29 begins a series of prophecies against Egypt (chs. 29–32). Like Tyre, Egypt is more strongly condemned than the other nations of the area. Egypt is condemned because of its history of political and military intrigue involving Judah.

PROPHECIES AGAINST EGYPT

In the sixteenth century BC, Egypt's influence extended to the Euphrates River in Mesopotamia. In the eighth century, Egypt opposed the rise of Assyria and backed Judah's rebellion against Assyria in 701 BC. However, Egypt proved time and again to be an ineffectual ally for Judah (Isaiah 30–31). Despite this history and the warnings of Jeremiah and Ezekiel, Jehoiakim (602 BC) and Zedekiah (598 BC) turned to Egypt for help against the Babylonians.

Egypt was of no help, offering only vain hopes for independence. The people of Israel were lured farther away from accepting God's will for them.

Thus, Ezekiel is called to proclaim disaster for Egypt and for Israel. He must expose the human folly of pride and self-reliance. He proclaims that the word of God controls all peoples and will not be evaded.

■ **Ezekiel 29:17-20.** Ezekiel's last dated prophecy was received on April 26, 571 BC. God tells Ezekiel that God is giving Egypt to Nebuchadnezzar as compensation for being God's agent against Tyre (586–573 BC; see Ezekiel 26:7). Nebuchadnezzar fought Tyre for thirteen years, but apparently received no appropriate spoils for his trouble. When a negotiated settlement was arranged, Tyre probably had no riches left after so long a siege.

Tyrian and Phoenician power declined after this defeat. Tyre remained an active trading and shipping center, but lost its dominant position on the coast. Today Tyre is a small town called Sur with about 6,000 inhabitants.

Amasis (569–525 BC), a young relative of Hophra, revolted against Pharaoh and took over the throne in 569 BC. Hophra was killed during the revolt, just as Jeremiah had prophesied. Nebuchadnezzar invaded Egypt (568–567 BC) and claimed victory over the Egyptian army. After this military campaign, Egypt was apparently no longer a threat to Nebuchadnezzar.

■ **Ezekiel 30.** Chapter 30 contains four poetic prophecies against Egypt (vv. 1-19) and one prose prophecy (vv. 20-26). Verses 1-19 are not dated. Verses 20-26 are dated April 29,

587 BC, during the Babylonian siege of Jerusalem. This was about one year after Pharaoh Hophra's unsuccessful attempt to break the siege.

■ **Ezekiel 30:1-8.** This first prophecy has the full introductory (vv. 1-2a) and concluding (v. 8a) phrases typical of prophetic announcements of judgment. One ancient manuscript omits the introductory phrase in verse 6 ("This is what the Lord says"). Verses 1-8 are presented as a single prophecy. Other translations retain the phrase and divide the verses into two prophecies (vv. 1-5, 6-9). Some regard all of verses 1-19 as the work of an editor later than Ezekiel. Other commentators believe verses 1-8 to be original to Ezekiel and verses 9-19 to be editorial expansions.

■ **Ezekiel 30:9.** This verse may be an editorial expansion. It recalls some of the same elements expressed in Ezekiel 7:5-9, of the day of the Lord. The proclamation "for it is sure to come" is very close to the "See, it comes" of Ezekiel 7:5.

This verse of prose between the poetry of verse 8 and verse 10 elaborates on how Egypt's doom will affect its ally, Ethiopia (Cush).

■ **Ezekiel 30:10-12.** This prophecy identifies the agent of Egypt's destruction as Nebuchadnezzar (Ezekiel 26:7). The king of Babylon and his armies will wield God's sword against Egypt.

The Nile is the source of life for Egypt. The dry Nile is a symbol of literal and figurative death for Egypt. Other natural phenomena are elsewhere proclaimed as part of the day of the Lord (Amos 8:9; Ezekiel 30:18).

■ **Ezekiel 30:14-15.** "Zoan" was an important commercial and military city in the Nile Delta on Egypt's eastern frontier.

"Thebes" was the center for the worship of the Egyptian god, Amon. It was a leading city in "Upper Egypt." It was the capital of the country during its periods of political unity from the Middle Kingdom (2000 BC) to the Assyrian invasion in approximately 661 BC, when the city was sacked.

"Pelusium" was near the mouth of the easternmost branch of the Nile. That would be west of the Suez Canal

PROPHECIES AGAINST EGYPT

and one mile from the Mediterranean. The city was known for its wine, and was an important military post on Egypt's eastern frontier.

■ **Ezekiel 30:17.** The Greek city of "Heliopolis" ("On" in the NRSV) is the modern Tell Husn. It is in lower Egypt, northwest of Cairo. This city was a famous center for the worship of the Egyptian sun-god, Ra.

"Bubastis" ("Pi-beseth" in the NRSV) is a city in the Nile Delta, southeast of present-day Zagazig. The Bible mentions this city only this one time. It was known for its celebrations in honor of the cat-headed goddess, Bastet.

■ **Ezekiel 30:18.** "Tahpanhes" ("Tehaphnehes" in the NRSV) is on the eastern frontier of lower Egypt, southwest of Pelusium. Refugees from Judah came to this fortress city to escape the Babylonians (Jeremiah 43:7), despite Jeremiah's prophecies against it (Jeremiah 42:19). Jeremiah later joined these refugees, prophesying destruction for them and for Egypt.

■ **Ezekiel 30:19.** The fall of these centers of human wealth and power is a testimony to the power of God. God will override the nations. God's passion is to be known and acknowledged by all people.

■ **Ezekiel 30:20-26.** This prophecy is dated April 29, 587 BC, about three months before Jerusalem falls to the Babylonian army. Ezekiel announces that, though Egypt may yet appear with one strong arm for battle, its fate is sealed. Neither those in Jerusalem nor the exiles should look to Egypt for help against the Babylonians.

■ **Ezekiel 31.** On June 21, 587 BC, Ezekiel receives a word from God to address the pharaoh of Egypt and his people. The first part of the address is an allegorical poem. The poem describes Egypt as a great tree, just as Tyre is described as a great ship (Ezekiel 27). The second and third parts of this address (vv. 10-14, 15-18) are prose. They proclaim the fall of the tree and its descent into Sheol.

This allegory describes no ordinary tree. Great trees are found in Mesopotamian, Teutonic, Indian, and Chinese religions. This tree symbolizes universal life. Its branches are in heaven and its roots are nourished by the waters of the primeval deep.

■ **Ezekiel 31:6.** The birds and beasts sheltered by the tree continue the symbolism of the universal life-giving tree. That "all the great nations" dwell in its shadow illustrates Egypt's power and wealth in relation to its neighbors. Ezekiel plainly uses this allegory to explain and forecast human history.

■ **Ezekiel 31:7-8.** None of the trees of Eden could compare with the beauty and greatness of this tree. The splendor of Egypt is unique.

A "plane" tree has large leaves, shedding bark, and spreading branches. Jacob uses branches of this tree to trick Laban in Haran (Genesis 30:37).

■ **Ezekiel 31:15.** In death, the tree will go to "the realm of the dead," the pit (28:8-10; 26:20). The deep that nurtured it will mourn its passing. The Nile that literally sustains Egypt will dry up (30:12). Its "abundant waters were restrained" by the deep that, figuratively, sustains the Egypt-tree (31:4). The destructive forces of nature and the destructive forces of human beings (30:25) will be brought to bear against Egypt.

Lebanon will be darkened or blackened in mourning. The trees of the field (other nations) will faint or veil their heads in mourning.

■ **Ezekiel 32.** The date of the first prophecy in chapter 32 is March 3, 585 BC. Ezekiel is directed to raise a lament over Pharaoh (vv. 2-8) as he raised one over the king of Tyre (28:11-19). A prophecy follows that identifies the agent of Egypt's downfall and is also a lament (vv. 11-16).

The final prophecy of the chapter (vv. 17-32) is dated April 27, 586 BC, nearly a year prior to verses 2-16. Ezekiel is commanded to wail in lamentation over Egypt's descent into the pit.

■ **Ezekiel 32:16.** The implication of Egypt's fall is that all peoples should learn from it. The lesson for the heathen and for the exiles is that the one God of history will have absolute power.

PROPHECIES AGAINST EGYPT

The "daughters of the nations" may include professional female mourners (2 Samuel 1:24; Jeremiah 9:17-18).

■ **Ezekiel 32:17-32.** Ezekiel is to wail over Egypt and to speak of what lies in store for it after death. Those who were uncircumcised, who were executed by the sword, or who died dishonorably and were not properly buried, were put in a separate place for the unclean. They were kept apart from the righteous dead. Both the circumstances of life and the treatment of the dead body affect the lot of a person in the nether world.

Ezekiel adds a moral dimension to this view of life and death. He feels the guilty in this life must pay in the life to come (v. 32). Thus, the pharaoh (and all Egypt) would normally be accorded the treatment in the afterlife due his status in earthly life. Now they will be confined to a place of dishonor in the pit (as is the Babylonian king in Isaiah 14:18-19).

■ **Ezekiel 32:19-21.** As in Isaiah 14:10, the fallen ones are greeted by those who have preceded them to the pit. Egypt is greeted with an ironic question reflecting Ezekiel 31:2b, 8c. The rest of the dead then confirm God's judgment. Egypt must lie with the dishonored ones in the shadowy and comfortless outer regions of the pit.

The "mighty leaders" may be the "warriors" of verse 27, who lie in a place of honor.

■ **Ezekiel 32:22-30.** In the underworld, Egypt is to join other nations who were also defeated through God's judgment. Assyria, Elam (a province of the Persian Empire), Meshek, Tubal (27:13), Edom (25:12-14), Sidon (28:20-33), and the princes of the north (rulers of Phoenicia and Syria) were all foes of Israel at one time or another.

■ **Ezekiel 32:31-32.** Perhaps Pharaoh will comfort himself with the fact that he is not the only mighty one who was banished to a dishonorable resting place in death.

Both verses 31 and 32 end with "declares the Sovereign LORD." This closing phrase is typical of prophetic announcements of judgment. This double ending indicates that there is more than one stage in the development of the written form of this prophecy.

DIMENSION THREE: WHAT DOES THE BIBLE MEAN TO ME?

Ezekiel 32—Ezekiel's Message of Lament

The situations in which the prophets carried out their ministry influenced the manner and form of their speech. These situations also influenced other aspects of their ministry and life. Their situation in life was characterized by social, political, and religious turning points or crises for the people of Israel. The prophets worked in times when Israel's choice, to obey or disobey the word of God, had become urgent.

Ezekiel lived and worked in such a time. He did not bring a totally new message in a completely new way. He used the tradition he was familiar with to formulate God's message. He appropriated some traditional forms of speech and traditional literary forms. He then gave these forms the character they needed to meet the needs of the moment. An example of this adaptation is found in Ezekiel's use of the lament in chapter 32.

How does our knowledge of Jesus and of the New Testament affect our understanding of Ezekiel's message? How does this knowledge affect our adaptation of his message for our time? Are there any limits on how we may enlarge or adapt Ezekiel's message? If so, what are these limits?

Do you think we know more about God than Ezekiel did? Does our knowledge of the revelation of Jesus affect our knowledge of God? Would Ezekiel know more about God in some ways than we do? Why? In what ways would his encounter with God be different from ours?

These questions are intended to you more aware of the multifaceted revelation of God in Scripture through the ages. They should also help you think about our process for adapting a message to our own situations and age. From what perspective do we approach Scripture? How do we adapt the Bible to our lives? In what ways does that make us more (or less) faithful to God?

I will make a covenant of peace with them. . . .
I will send down showers in season. (34:25-26)

RESTORATION AND FULFILLMENT

Ezekiel 33–39

DIMENSION ONE: WHAT DOES THE BIBLE SAY?

Answer these questions by reading Ezekiel 33

1. Whom does God call to be a watchman for Israel? (33:7)

2. What is the watchman to do? (33:3, 9)

3. When does Ezekiel hear that Jerusalem has fallen? (33:21)

4. Even though the people come to listen to Ezekiel, why will they be punished? (33:31-32)

Answer these questions by reading Ezekiel 34

5. Why does Ezekiel prophesy against the shepherds of Israel? (34:3-4, 8)

6. Who are the sheep? (34:30-31)

7. Who are the shepherds? (34:23)

Answer these questions by reading Ezekiel 35

8. Against whom does Ezekiel prophesy? (35:2, 15)

9. Why is Edom to be punished? (35:5, 12)

Answer these questions by reading Ezekiel 36

10. What does God promise will happen to Israel's neighbors? (36:6-7)

11. What does God promise will happen to the people of Israel? (36:8-11)

12. Why will God gather the people into their own land again? (36:22-24)

13. How will God change the people once they are in their own land again? (36:26-29)

Answer these questions by reading Ezekiel 37

14. What question does God ask Ezekiel as he sees the valley of dry bones? (37:3)

RESTORATION AND FULFILLMENT

15. How will the bones live? (37:4-6)

16. Who are the bones? (37:11)

17. Why is Ezekiel to join the stick of Judah with the stick of Joseph? (37:18-22)

Answer these questions by reading Ezekiel 38

18. Against whom does Ezekiel now prophesy? (38:2)

19. When will Gog move against Israel? (38:8, 14)

20. What will happen to Gog? (38:21)

Answer these questions by reading Ezekiel 39

21. Who will lead Gog to his destruction in the mountains of Israel? (39:1-2)

22. Why does God lead Gog to his destruction? (39:7, 21-22)

23. Why will the Israelites know that the Lord is their God? (39:28-29)

DIMENSION TWO: WHAT DOES THE BIBLE MEAN?

■ **Ezekiel 33.** Verses 1-20 speak of Ezekiel's responsibility as a watchman for Israel. They also speak of an individual's responsibility for his or her own wicked or righteous living. Verses 21-22 tell of the messenger coming to Ezekiel in January 586 BC, from Jerusalem. He brings the news of Jerusalem's fall to the Babylonians. Verses 23-33 tell of the folly of those left in Israel and of the exiles in Babylon as well.

■ **Ezekiel 33:10-16.** In this prophecy, God anticipates the reaction of the people to Ezekiel's message. Apparently, they understand that their sins have led them to the point of death. Yet, in confessing their sin, they do not seem to understand that death is not inevitable. They must take a hand in saving themselves.

In verse 11 God states positively, "I take no pleasure in the death of the wicked." In Ezekiel 18:23 this is stated as a rhetorical question. God's will is to redeem the people.

■ **Ezekiel 33:23-29.** This prophecy comes from the time after the Babylonians had burned Jerusalem. Attempts were being made to bring the land of Judah into some type of order again. These verses may reflect the efforts of Gedaliah to resettle the scattered population before he was assassinated (Jeremiah 40:13–41:18).

■ **Ezekiel 33:30-33.** Here, God does not tell Ezekiel to issue a prophetic word. God warns Ezekiel about those who come to listen to his messages. Despite their loving words, they are concerned only for their own gain.

"When all this comes true" may refer to the specific judgment announced in verses 23-29. The phrase may also refer to a more general fulfillment of God's word on the day of the Lord. God promises Ezekiel that, though his message may be maligned or misunderstood, it will be victorious (12:3).

■ **Ezekiel 34:7-8.** "Therefore" may indicate that these verses are a later addition. They merely repeat the prophecy given

RESTORATION AND FULFILLMENT

in verses 3-6. The oath, "as surely as I live," adds a note of certainty to the punishment.

■ **Ezekiel 34:11-16.** These verses carry on the theme of God's intervention on behalf of the flock. The imagery of shepherd and flock is mixed with the reality of God and people.

The "day of clouds and darkness" suggests the day of the Lord.

■ **Ezekiel 34:17-19.** God accuses some of the sheep of taking advantage of the rest of the flock. God will purge the bad sheep from the flock (20:33-38).

■ **Ezekiel 35.** Chapter 35 contains prophetic announcements of judgment against Edom. In content, they belong with the other prophecies against foreign nations, especially Ezekiel 25:12-14. Their present position in the book comes from their relationship to chapter 36. In chapters 35 and 36:1-15, the threats against Israel's enemy Edom intensify the promises of hope for Israel.

Israel and Edom have a long history of animosity. This animosity began while the Israelites were wandering in the desert (Numbers 20:14-21). Later, David conquered Edom (2 Samuel 8:13-14).

Edomites began moving into southern Judah after 587 BC, when Arabian tribes pushed them from their own lands (Jeremiah 49:17-22). This migration led to growing Judean hatred for these neighbors who were once their brothers (Deuteronomy 23:7-8).

■ **Ezekiel 36.** The "mountains of Israel" (all of Israel) are addressed here with prophecies of hope for themselves and destruction for the enemy.

■ **Ezekiel 36:1-15.** These verses appear to be a composite of several short messages set off by "this is what the Sovereign LORD says." The nations surrounding Israel are the enemy.

■ **Ezekiel 36:17-19.** God accuses Israel of impurity. Israel's uncleanness is compared to the biblical understanding of a woman's uncleanness during menstruation (Ezekiel 18:6; Leviticus 15:19-30). He repeats the charges of injustice (Ezekiel 7:23) and idolatry (Ezekiel 6:1-4).

■ **Ezekiel 36:20-21.** Israel's faithfulness and prosperity were to be a testimony to the power of God. The people's unfaithfulness and punishment have caused the heathen to question this power.

■ **Ezekiel 36:22-23.** "Therefore" God will act on Israel's behalf.

■ **Ezekiel 36:24-32.** God describes how Israel will be delivered.

■ **Ezekiel 36:31-32.** These verses pull verses 16-23 and 24-32 together. Israel must remember its past sins. In remembering, the people must focus their new life on God and God's goodness.

■ **Ezekiel 36:33-36, 37-38.** These verses fill out the promises of restoration given in verses 24-32. They repeat some of the specifics of verses 8-11. God's name will not be profaned in the sight of the nations (v. 21).

The "people" of verse 37 is translated from the Hebrew word *adam* that means "human being." The word can mean an individual or humankind as a whole.

■ **Ezekiel 37:1-14:** This is the well-known story of the valley of dry bones. In a vision, Ezekiel is transported to a valley, where God calls on him to prophesy to the dry bones that fill the valley. In a vivid demonstration of God's sovereignty and the power of divine prophecy, the bones not only come together, but are connected by tendons and covered with flesh. Through Ezekiel's prophecy, God then breathes life into the bones.

■ **Ezekiel 37:15-17.** *Judah* represents the Southern Kingdom; *Joseph*, the name of its leading tribe, represents the Northern Kingdom. *Ephraim* is used elsewhere to designate the northern tribes.

The name *Israel* is used to represent the people as a whole.

■ **Ezekiel 37:18-22.** Ezekiel interprets his actions. God's complete plan for the people includes those of the north, who had been absorbed by Assyria in 722 BC. God also has plans for those in the south, who are in Babylon. The long-standing enmity between the two will cease.

RESTORATION AND FULFILLMENT

- **Ezekiel 37:23-24.** God's people will live within the covenant. David (or a Davidic king), God's servant/shepherd (34:26), will be their leader.
- **Ezekiel 37:27-28.** God's sanctuary is God's dwelling place with the people. The sanctuary is a symbol of Israel's new relationship to God. Other nations now have a sign that Israel is again sanctified by the power of God.
- **Ezekiel 38–39.** These two chapters are a series of prophecies against Gog, a foe from the north who comes against the reunited kingdom of Israel.

These prophecies are placed between the promises of a new sanctuary for Israel in Ezekiel 37:28 and Ezekiel's vision of its fulfillment in chapters 40–48.

- **Ezekiel 38:24.** *Magog* may mean "land of Gog." Gog will be used for God's purposes. The images of hooks are similar to those in 19:4 and 29:4.
- **Ezekiel 38:6.** Gomer invaded Asia Minor in the eighth century BC.
- **Ezekiel 38:7-9.** The promises of 37:15-28 have been fulfilled. "After many days . . . In future years" refers to the time elapsed. During this time, Israel has settled once more in the Promised Land.
- **Ezekiel 38:10-13.** Jerusalem is the center of the earth (Ezekiel 5:5). Sheba, Dedan, and Tarshish see Gog's plan as an opportunity to ally with him.
- **Ezekiel 39:11.** The dead must be buried to cleanse the land (Numbers 35:33). The "valley of those who travel east of] the Sea" is in the mountains of northern Moab. Israel had lost this territory to Moab, and it is not included in the limits of the new Israel given in Ezekiel 40–48.

The impurity of the burial place in the valley may keep travelers from passing through. The "Valley of Hamon Gog" means "the Valley of the Multitude of Gog."

- **Ezekiel 39:25-29.** These verses summarize God's acts of salvation for the house of Israel from chapters 34–37. They reintroduce the themes that were developed before the

Gog prophecies. They make a transition into the final great vision in chapters 40–48.

Israel will continue to be blessed by the outpouring of God's Spirit as it guarantees a right relationship between God and people.

DIMENSION THREE: WHAT DOES THE BIBLE MEAN TO ME?

Ezekiel 36:22-32—Cleansing and Renewal

This passage elaborates on a promise made by God to the people. Here God is reminding the people that, through cleansing, they will be restored. After their restoration, they will be a sign for all the nations of the glory of God.

In the Christian religious tradition, cleansing is symbolized by baptism. Baptism denotes inclusion in the body of Christ and freedom from guilt.

Without an acceptance of an inward change by the one being cleansed, the ritual itself is empty. Yet, in a sense, the ritual does carry an active power to consummate and symbolize the change.

What has baptism meant to you in your faith journey? How else can we be cleansed from sin? When have you received a new heart after being cleansed? Does cleansing always bring renewal? Why or why not?

Ezekiel 34:17-22—Sheep and Goats

In this passage, the prophet is using the familiar imagery of sheep and goats to speak of the people of Israel. To continue the imagery, God is the shepherd of Israel.

Ezekiel's message is that the sheep (people) must be in right relationships with one another. Only then will they be in a right relationship with their shepherd, God. Think about the times in your life when you have not been in a right relationship with another person. Did this situation relate to your relationship to God? How?

I looked and saw the glory of the LORD filling the temple of the LORD, and I fell facedown. (44:4)

VISION OF THE RESTORED TEMPLE
Ezekiel 40–44

DIMENSION ONE: WHAT DOES THE BIBLE SAY?

Answer these questions by reading Ezekiel 40

1. When does Ezekiel receive the vision of the restored Temple? (40:1)

2. Why is Ezekiel shown this vision? (40:4)

3. What does the man do with a linen cord and a measuring rod? (40:3, 5-14a)

4. In which directions do the gates face? (40:6, 20, 24)

5. For whom were the rooms next to the north and south gates? (40:44-46)

Answer these questions by reading Ezekiel 41

6. Where is the Most Holy Place in the Temple? (41:1-4)

7. How long are the Temple and its courtyard on each side? (41:13-15)

8. What figures are carved on the walls and doors of the inner room and outer sanctuary? (41:17-25)

9. What do these cherubim look like? (41:18-19)

Answer these questions by reading Ezekiel 42

10. How are the priests to use the holy rooms on the north and south sides of the Temple? (42:13)

11. What should the priests do before they go to the outer court of the Temple? (42:14)

12. How long is each side of the Temple area "all around"? (42:16-19)

13. Why is there a wall around the Temple? (42:20)

VISION OF THE RESTORED TEMPLE

Answer these questions by reading Ezekiel 43

14. To what does Ezekiel compare the vision he sees at the Temple? (43:1-3)

15. What does Ezekiel see filling the Temple? (43:5)

16. What is God's relationship to the new Temple? (43:7)

17. Why is Ezekiel to describe the Temple? (43:10)

18. For what does God give the dimensions and the regulations for its use in the Temple? (43:13-27)

19. Who is to minister to God in the Temple? (43:19)

Answer these questions by reading Ezekiel 44

20. Why is the east gate of the Temple to remain shut? (44:1-2)

21. Why are foreigners to be excluded from the Temple? (44:6-8)

22. Why are the sons of Zadok, of all the Levitical priests, allowed full ministry in the Temple? (44:15)

23. What will the conduct and lifestyle of the priests teach the Lord's people? (44:23)

DIMENSION TWO: WHAT DOES THE BIBLE MEAN?

Chapters 40–48 of Ezekiel are a great vision report. They tell of the Temple, the land, and the people in the time of restoration and fulfillment that God plans for Israel.

■ **Ezekiel 40.** The vision of the reconstructed Temple in Jerusalem is found in Ezekiel 40:1–42:20. This Temple is essentially like Solomon's Temple, which was burned in August of 587 BC by the Babylonians. Ezekiel may have served in this first Temple as a priest before the Exile. Chapter 40 describes the gates, and the inner and outer courts of the Temple.

■ **Ezekiel 40:7, 10, 12-13.** The heavenly guide ("a man whose appearance was like bronze") measures the rooms on either side, inside the gateway (each is about ten feet square). The guide also measures the threshold at the inner end of the gateway. The side rooms are probably used by priests who keep watch over those who enter the Temple. The barrier (v. 12) may be like the rim around the altar base (43:13).

■ **Ezekiel 40:20-27.** The northern and southern gates into the outer court are similar to the eastern gate. All of the gates through the outer wall into the outer court are inspected before the gates into the inner court.

■ **Ezekiel 40:28-37.** Ezekiel is shown the three gates leading in to the inner court. Eight steps lead up from the outer court to the gateways of the inner court. The Temple building itself is on top of a series of terraces.

The inner gateways are the same as the outer ones except that the order of porticoes and side rooms is reversed. The portico is nearest the entrance steps (v. 31). The east and north gates are the same.

- **Ezekiel 41:1-2.** The "main hall" is the outer sanctuary of the Temple. Its length and width are the same as those of Solomon's Temple (1 Kings 6:2-3, 17).
- **Ezekiel 41:34.** Only the guide goes into the "inner sanctuary," the Most Holy Place (or Holy of Holies); the ark of the covenant is not mentioned. As a priest, Ezekiel is allowed to enter the outer sanctuary. But he does not go into the Most Holy Place. After the Exile, the Most Holy Place is entered only once a year by the high priest on the Day of Atonement.

The Temple is divided into three parts: the portico, the outer sanctuary, and the Most Holy Place. As in the preceding verses (except vv. 38-46), the essential outline of the Temple is given with few elaborating details.

- **Ezekiel 42:1-14.** These verses describe the priests' rooms on the northern and southern sides of the building, to the west of the Temple building. The details of the description are not clear. Apparently, the rooms are built in three rows, terraced against the slope that rises from the outer court up to the Temple level.

The priests use these rooms to cook (46:19-20) and eat their meals. They also store their share of the sacrifices here (44:28-31) and change from the holy garments they wear for services into the common garments. "The priests who approach the Lord" (v. 13) are the Zadokites (43:19).

- **Ezekiel 43:7.** The reality of God's presence is expressed by proclaiming the Temple as the place of God's throne and of the soles of God's feet (see Jeremiah 14:21; 17:12; Lamentations 2:1; Psalm 132:7).

The "funeral offerings" may be memorial stones dedicated to past kings, some of whom may be unworthy. All respect and honor within the Temple must go to God.

- **Ezekiel 43:8-9.** "When they placed their threshold next to my threshold" may refer to royal tombs that were constructed to look like a house. It may also refer to the king's palace standing beside the Temple. Solomon's palace did not adjoin the Temple building, but was inside the outer court.

■ **Ezekiel 43:13-17.** The altar looks like a series of steps. It is built in three, superimposed squares resting on a foundation platform. The steps leading up to the altar face the east gate.

The "gutter on the ground" (v. 14) comes from the Hebrew meaning "bosom of the earth." The top of the altar, "the altar hearth" (v. 15), comes from an Akkadian word meaning "mountain of God."

The horns project from each corner of the altar hearth. They may be symbols of divinity. Holding onto these horns may offer protection to a fugitive.

■ **Ezekiel 43:18.** The altar must be cleansed. Throwing blood against the altar is part of an ancient covenant-making ritual (Exodus 24:6). The blood is thought to contain the life-force of an animal. Giving this blood back to God, the Giver of life, cleanses away sin.

■ **Ezekiel 43:19.** The family of Zadok is specified as the faithful line of priests who may assume authority in the new Temple (44:5-31).

■ **Ezekiel 44:10-14.** The foreigners serving in the Temple are to be replaced by Levites, who are to be punished. Perhaps they are being punished for worshiping in the high places. They will be put in charge of the duties of the Temple (guarding the gates, slaughtering the burnt offerings and serving the people), but may not approach the altar.

■ **Ezekiel 44:15-16.** Verse 15 may be a later addition. It contrasts the accusations of 7:26; 22:26; chapter 8. It may have been added by a disciple who was a Zadokite priest interested in establishing a dominant role for this line in the postexilic Temple and community.

The Zadokite priests are "alone are to enter my sanctuary; they alone are to come near my table to minister before me and serve me as guards" (v. 16). Zadokite priests may have descended from Jebusite priests, who were in Jerusalem before David captured the city. Zadok became high priest in Jerusalem under Solomon (1 Kings 1:26-27).

VISION OF THE RESTORED TEMPLE

The question of descent relates to authority and a struggle for power that continues after the exiles return to Israel.

"My table" is the table of the bread of the Presence.

DIMENSION THREE: WHAT DOES THE BIBLE MEAN TO ME?

Ezekiel 40–43—Ezekiel and God's Presence

Chapters 40–43 are part of the prophet's vision of the restored Temple and land. These chapters describe the Temple area, the gates, the outer courts, the Temple's general architecture, and the rooms in which the priests were to reside and do their work. The section ends with a description of the return of God's glory (see Ezekiel 43:1-12).

Ezekiel is relevant today for his challenge to smug attitudes about God's presence, God's Temple, and God's worship. Ezekiel urges people not to try to bind God or limit God. In other words, the people must be open to God's presence and revelation in whatever form or place God chooses. The Temple is but a sign of God's presence. It cannot and does not contain God entirely.

How do we as Christians experience God's presence? How is our experience different from Ezekiel's? Do we accept God's presence, but still try to limit God's power over us?

When you allot the land as an inheritance, you are to present the LORD a portion of the land as a sacred district. (45:1)

10
VISION OF THE RESTORED LAND
Ezekiel 45–48

DIMENSION ONE: WHAT DOES THE BIBLE SAY?

Answer these questions by reading Ezekiel 45

1. Why is a portion of land set aside for the Lord? (45:1)

2. What will be in this sacred district? (45:2-5)

3. What does God tell the princes of Israel to do? (45:8-9)

4. Why are the families of Israel instructed to make offerings to the Lord? (45:15)

Answer these questions by reading Ezekiel 46

5. On what occasions will the east gate of the Temple be opened? (46:1)

VISION OF THE RESTORED LAND

6. What are the people to do at the entrance of the open gate? (46:3)

7. How are the people to be protected from being dispossessed of their property? (46:18)

8. What are the priests to do in the kitchens? (46:20, 24)

Answer these questions by reading Ezekiel 47

9. What does Ezekiel see coming from below the threshold of the Temple? (47:1)

10. How does the water change as it flows farther from the Temple? (47:3-5)

11. Which way does the water flow? (47:8)

12. What special quality does the river possess? (47:9)

13. Why will the trees along the river flourish and bear much fruit? (47:12)

14. Among whom is the land to be divided? (47:21-23)

Answer these questions by reading Ezekiel 48

15. Beginning at the northern border of Israel, which are the first tribes assigned land? (48:1-7)

16. What portion adjoins the southern border of Judah's portion? (48:8-9)

17. Who gets the land to the east and west of the sacred portion and just south of the Temple portion? (48:15, 21)

18. What are the remaining tribes that are assigned portions of land? (48:23-27)

19. After whom are the gates of the New Jerusalem to be named? (48:31-34)

20. What new name is given the city? (48:35)

DIMENSION TWO: WHAT DOES THE BIBLE MEAN?

■ **Ezekiel 45.** Chapter 45 contains instructions for the distribution of land (vv. 1-8), for the duties of the prince (vv. 9-17), and for Temple purification and festivals (vv. 18-24).

■ **Ezekiel 45:7-8.** The prince is allotted land on either side of the central square. His portion is eight miles wide. It stretches east to the Jordan Valley and west to the Mediterranean Sea.

VISION OF THE RESTORED LAND

Verse 8 implies that the princes are given a large portion of land so they will no longer take land that belongs to the people. The verse also anticipates the further division of the land to the tribes in Ezekiel 47.

Here we have a transition from the division of the land to a rebuke of the princes, a set of regulations regarding weights, and the duties of the princes (vv. 10-17). God speaks in the first person rather than in the third person (v. 4). Also, God speaks of *princes* rather than *the prince* (vv. 7, 16).

■ **Ezekiel 45:9.** This verse echoes the command God gave to the house of Israel in 44:6. Apparently, these verses do not have in mind the shepherd/prince of 34:20-24 or 37:24-28. These princes must be warned against falling into the disobedience of former days (22:23-31).

■ **Ezekiel 46:1-3.** Inside the Temple compound, the eastern gate that leads into the inner court will be opened on the sabbath and "on the day of the New Moon." (In a lunar calendar this would be the first day of the month).

Neither the prince nor the people may enter the inner court. The prince may bring his offerings to the portico of the inner eastern gate (45:13-17). He will stand in the inner portico by the ritually cleansed doorway (45:18-19). There he will worship while the priests offer the sacrifices. The people must worship before the gateway in the outer court.

■ **Ezekiel 46:4-7.** The sacrifices ordered here differ from those in Numbers 28:9-15. The sabbath has as many animals for sacrifice as there are days of the week. Additional sacrifices are required for the new moon. The bull is associated with the moon in Babylonian hymns. It is a common symbol for fertility in the ancient Near East.

■ **Ezekiel 47:1-2.** The water originates from under the south wall of the Temple threshold. The water apparently disappears from sight. It then reappears, flowing from underneath the south wall of the eastern Temple gate in the outer wall. The guide leads Ezekiel out of the outer court through the northern gate because the eastern gate is kept closed (44:1-3).

The water is a blessing from God. It brings abundant life to desert wastelands and fresh water to the saline waters of the Dead Sea. It symbolizes new life for God's people through God's saving grace. This stream is reminiscent of the river of Eden. The river of Eden gives rise to four rivers that reach to the four corners of the ancient world. The water of God sustains life in the Promised Land. It flows as a result of God's dwelling once again in the midst of the people.

■ **Ezekiel 47:3-5.** In a little over a mile (1,000 cubits is approximately 568 yards), the water grows from an ankle-deep brook to a mighty river.

■ **Ezekiel 47:12.** This vision of a new paradise depends upon God's presence with the people. This holy presence renews all aspects of life, both inward and outward (36:26-28; 47:1-12). God's chosen people are to be returned to their homeland, which is to be transformed. This transformation goes beyond normal expectations of fruitfulness and security. God's mighty presence and the renewed relationship with the people are accompanied by a transformation of the land into a garden of paradise.

In this sense, the vision carries God's people into a state of salvation. This salvation cannot be achieved in human history as it has been known. This new state comes about through a divine new age. This new age, however, is not "otherworldly." It is grounded in Israel's history with God and is to be lived out in this world, in real time.

■ **Ezekiel 47:13–48:35.** The remainder of Ezekiel defines the boundaries of the new Israel and the division of the land.

■ **Ezekiel 47:21-23.** Before the actual division of the land among the tribes, provisions are made for foreigners who live among the Israelites. They had previously been given certain rights in Israel against oppression (Exodus 22:21-22). They could own houses and could become wealthy (Leviticus 25:4 7). They are to be treated as Israelites (Leviticus 19:34; Numbers 15:29). This passage is the only one that specifically grants foreigners the right to own land and to pass it on to their children.

VISION OF THE RESTORED LAND

■ **Ezekiel 48:1-7, 23-29.** The tribes are named after the sons of Jacob (Genesis 35:22-26), with Joseph's sons (Manasseh and Ephraim, vv. 4-5) named instead of Levi, the priestly tribe (see Ezekiel 47:13). Each tribe has an equal portion of land, stretching from the western to the eastern frontier. The length of these portions is 25,000 cubits, or eight and three-tenths miles (Ezekiel 45:1; 48:8). The width is not specified.

The allotments are made from north to south. The tribe of Dan is the farthest north. Next is the tribe of Asher, and then Naphtali. Gad, whose territory was formerly east of the Jordan, is assigned the portion farthest south (v. 27). These four tribes are assigned the territory that is farthest away from the sacred district and the Temple. This location may be because these four are named for sons of Jacob's concubines: Bilhah (Dan and Naphtali) and Zilpah (Gad and Asher), rather than for sons of Jacob's wives: Leah (Reuben, Simeon, Levi, Judah, Issachar, and Zebulun) and Rachel (Joseph and Benjamin).

The tribes of the wives' sons are closest to the sacred district. Judah and Benjamin are assigned favored positions on either side of the central strip. Formerly, Judah and Simeon were the tribes living south of Jerusalem.

Verse 28 describes the southern boundary (47:19). Verse 29 summarizes 47:13–48:28 and concludes with the phrase typically at the end of prophetic speeches.

DIMENSION THREE: WHAT DOES THE BIBLE MEAN TO ME?

Ezekiel the Man

Ezekiel was from a priestly family and probably trained for the priesthood. He was a husband, living in exile with his wife and possibly other members of his family. He received his call to prophesy with agitation and fear. But he was true to his commitment to serve as God needed him.

Ezekiel suffered misunderstanding from his people, physical discomfort, and personal grief during his ministry. Yet he was a man of intellect who could speak and write effectively.

We really know little about him as a person, or about his history. Yet he would probably find this appropriate. The message, not the man, is foremost in his prophecy. Reflect on what you have learned about Ezekiel the man during the past ten lessons.

Now, think about what Ezekiel has taught us about God. What has this book taught you about your own faith? Your relationships with other persons?

To these four young men God gave knowledge and understanding of all kinds of literature and learning. And Daniel could understand visions and dreams of all kinds. (1:17)

11

GOD'S SERVANTS IN BABYLON

Daniel 1–4

DIMENSION ONE: WHAT DOES THE BIBLE SAY?

Answer these questions by reading Daniel 1

1. When does Nebuchadnezzar besiege Jerusalem? (1:1)

2. Who gives Jehoiakim and Judah into Nebuchadnezzar's hand? (1:2)

3. Who are the young men of Judah given special attention by Nebuchadnezzar? (1:6)

4. How do these four differ from the other young men? (1:11-16)

5. How does God help these young men? (1:17)

6. How long does Daniel stay in Nebuchadnezzar's kingdom? (1:21)

Answer these questions by reading Daniel 2

7. Why is Nebuchadnezzar troubled? (2:3)

8. What does Nebuchadnezzar demand of his astrologers? (2:5-6)

9. What does Daniel do when the astrologers cannot meet the king's demands? (2:16)

10. How is the mystery revealed to Daniel? (2:17-19)

11. In Daniel's interpretation, what does the "large statue" represent? (2:31, 36-43)

12. What is the rock that strikes the statue? (2:44-45)

13. How does Nebuchadnezzar react to Daniel's interpretation? (2:47-49)

Answer these questions by reading Daniel 3

14. What does Nebuchadnezzar make for all the people to worship? (3:1)

GOD'S SERVANTS IN BABYLON

15. Who refuses to worship the image? (3:12)

16. What is their punishment? (3:22-23)

17. How do the three men survive the fire? (3:25, 28)

18. Why does God save them? (3:28)

19. What does Nebuchadnezzar learn about God from this experience? (3:29)

Answer these questions by reading Daniel 4

20. What does Nebuchadnezzar want to tell all peoples? (4:2)

21. To whom does Nebuchadnezzar turn for an interpretation of his dream? (4:8, 18)

22. Who does Daniel say is the tree of Nebuchadnezzar's dream? (4:22)

23. Why is Nebuchadnezzar to be driven away? (4:25)

24. What happens to Nebuchadnezzar because of his pride and boasting? (4:32-33)

25. What does Nebuchadnezzar do when he regains his reason? (4:34-37)

DIMENSION TWO: WHAT DOES THE BIBLE MEAN?

■ **Daniel 1.** Chapter 1 introduces us to Daniel and explains how he happens to be in Babylon. It establishes Daniel's character of faithfulness and wisdom. The story is self-contained and told in the third person.

■ **Daniel 1:6-7.** The name *Daniel* is common to this time. Its spelling varies, changing its meaning. In Ezekiel, the Hebrew spelling used (*Danel*) means "God is judge" (Ezekiel 14:14, 20). In the Book of Daniel, it means "God is my judge."

The Babylonian officer gives Babylonian names to the Hebrew young men. This naming marks a transition into a new rank and life. Names such as these are known in Akkadian and agree with what is known about Akkadian names from the sixth century BC. The Akkadians were among the earliest Semitic settlers in Mesopotamia. Assyrian and Babylonian are Akkadian dialects.

■ **Daniel 1:17-21.** Again, the storyteller points out that God is the source of wisdom and understanding for the four Hebrew young men. From the Babylonians, they may have learned the literature and languages of other nations, astrology, astronomy, mathematics, and medicine.

Daniel and his friends are more knowledgeable than all the magicians and exorcists in Babylon. Wisdom given by God is always "ten times better" than human wisdom alone. The number ten is used in verse 20 in a symbolic sense to represent completeness.

■ **Daniel 2.** Chapter 2 tells the story of Daniel's skill in telling and interpreting dreams. As in chapter 1, his skill is attributed to God and to his asking God for discernment. This story stands on its own. But it assumes the reader has read the first story and knows who the main characters are.

- **Daniel 2:3-11.** In verse 4, the Hebrew reads, "Then the Chaldeans said to the king in Aramaic." The rest of verse 4 and on through Daniel 7:28 is written in Aramaic. Aramaic is an ancient Semitic language; it was the international language of the ancient Near East by the eighth century BC. Because the language grew and changed with time, it is divided into classes. "Official Aramaic" was in use from, approximately, 730 to 300 BC. Recent linguistic evidence suggests that the Aramaic of Daniel is of this type.
- **Daniel 2:27-38.** Nebuchadnezzar's kingdom is represented by the head of gold. Nebuchadnezzar holds power at God's dispensation. Like Jeremiah and Ezekiel, Daniel regards Nebuchadnezzar and the rest of the non-Hebrew world as being under God's control.
- **Daniel 2:39.** The second kingdom may be either the Medo-Persian or the Median kingdom. Daniel refers to the Medes and Persians together (5:28; 6:9) and separately (9:1).

  The third kingdom may be the Persians or the Greeks.
- **Daniel 2:40-43.** The fourth kingdom may be either the Greek or the Roman Empire. Alexander the Great of Greece defeated the Persians in 333 BC. At his death in 323 BC, his empire was divided among his generals. Verse 43 refers to marriages between the ruling families. The fifth kingdom is God's, represented by a mountain.

  We must keep in mind the overall symbolism of the statue and not focus only on the specifics of what each part may represent. In one sense, the statue represents all vestiges of human power that will be overwhelmed and replaced by God's power. Even though the statue represents successive kingdoms, the whole statue falls and is broken at the same time.
- **Daniel 2:44-45.** Some see the fifth kingdom, the mountain of God, as the coming of Christ. Daniel's visions are borne out by history, but still hold the prospect of further fulfillment, which some people believe is the Second Coming of Christ.

  The rock cut "not by human hands" reflects the mountain/kingdom of God (Genesis 28:10-22; 49:24; Psalm 118:22; Isaiah 28:16). For us as Christians, the rock may be seen to anticipate the cornerstone (Matthew 21:42; Mark 12:10; Luke 20:17; Acts 4:11; Ephesians 2:20-21; 1 Peter 2:6, 7).

■ **Daniel 3:2.** The word *satrap* comes from an old Persian word meaning "protector of the realm." A satrap was the head official in a province. The use of this word in Daniel suggests that the book was written before 300 BC.

Nebuchadnezzar may have wanted these officials to affirm publicly their loyalty to him by worshiping the image of his deity. Nebuchadnezzar suppressed a revolt in his tenth year as king. Zedekiah's visit to Babylon in 593 BC may have been required by Nebuchadnezzar to reaffirm Zedekiah's loyalty to him (see Jeremiah 51:59-64).

■ **Daniel 3:24-25.** Nebuchadnezzar looks into the furnace at ground level. Shadrach, Meshach, and Abednego are walking around. The fourth man is a heavenly being or angel (v. 28). The Talmud identifies him as the archangel Gabriel.

■ **Daniel 3:26-28.** Nebuchadnezzar acknowledges the power of God as he calls the men out of the furnace. Note that he calls God "the Most High God," not the only god. Nebuchadnezzar is still a polytheist.

■ **Daniel 4.** This chapter is a proclamation or letter by Nebuchadnezzar to the people of his realm. Within this proclamation he tells of a dream he had, of its interpretation, and of its fulfillment. He attributes all that happens to him (including madness and restoration!) to "the Most High God." The purpose of his proclamation is to tell of "the miraculous signs and wonders" (v. 2) of the Most High God and to offer praise to God. This communication from a powerful ruler to his people is astonishing in its honesty and humility.

DIMENSION THREE: WHAT DOES THE BIBLE MEAN TO ME?

Daniel 4—Confession and Praise

Chapter 4 tells the story of Nebuchadnezzar's madness. The purpose of this story is to help us realize that even a great power such as the king of Babylon is helpless in the face of the power of God.

Nebuchadnezzar begins and ends his proclamation by praising God (vv. 2-3, 34-35). His sin, punishment, and restoration are told in the context of praise and confession. The phrase "my sanity was restored" occurs in verses 34 and 36. Whether Nebuchadnezzar's return to sanity preceded his praise of God, or whether the two coincided, is unclear. Whatever the case, praise is involved in bringing the sinner back into right relationship to God.

Think about the times in your life when you have experienced deliverance from sin or from a serious problem in your life. How did you respond in these situations? Did you praise God as Nebuchadnezzar did?

Daniel 1-4—Godly Wisdom

The stories in Daniel are told from a perspective of faith in God. They inform us about a part of the history of our faith. They teach lessons about God and about God's relationships to human beings. They do this by dramatically relating particular human experiences with God. The stories in and of themselves are interesting. However, their real significance lies in the fact that we recognize Daniel's God as our God.

Think back over what you have learned in studying the first four chapters in the Book of Daniel. What does Daniel teach us about the nature of God? Share your thoughts with other group members.

What proverbs or wise sayings are illustrated by the stories in the first four chapters of Daniel? Compose your own proverb or wisdom saying to summarize what these stories as a whole, or each story individually, teach you.

For he is the living God / and he endures forever; / his kingdom will not be destroyed, / his dominion will never end.
(6:26)

12
HUMAN DESTINY, DIVINE CONTROL
Daniel 5–8

DIMENSION ONE: WHAT DOES THE BIBLE SAY?

Answer these questions by reading Daniel 5

1. Who is now king of Babylon? (5:1-2)

2. What does he do with the goblets from the Jerusalem Temple? (5:2-4)

3. What happens after they drink and offer praise? (5:5)

4. Who interprets the writing? (5:17)

5. Why does the hand appear with a message? (5:18-23)

HUMAN DESTINY, DIVINE CONTROL

6. What is Belshazzar's punishment? (5:26-28, 30-31)

Answer these questions by reading Daniel 6

7. Why do the other administrators and satraps plot against Daniel? (6:3)

8. How do they plan to get the king to dispose of Daniel? (6:6-9)

9. What happens to Daniel? (6:10-18)

10. Who saves Daniel from the lions? (6:19-22)

11. How does Darius respond to God after this? (6:25-27)

12. What happens to Daniel after this? (6:28)

Answer these questions by reading Daniel 7

13. What does this chapter tell about? (7:1)

14. What does Daniel see come up from the great sea? (7:3)

15. Who takes a seat on the throne? (7:9)

16. To whom is presented a kingdom "that will never be destroyed"? (7:13-14)

17. How does Daniel interpret the vision? (7:16)

18. What is the interpretation? (7:17-18)

19. Why is the fourth beast different from the rest? (7:23-26)

Answer these questions by reading Daniel 8

20. When does Daniel receive this vision? (8:1)

21. What two animals does Daniel see in the vision? (8:3-12)

22. Who interprets the vision for Daniel? (8:15-16)

23. What is the vision about? (8:17, 19, 26)

24. Who do the animals represent? (8:20-21)

25. How does Daniel react to the vision? (8:27)

HUMAN DESTINY, DIVINE CONTROL

DIMENSION TWO: WHAT DOES THE BIBLE MEAN?

■ **Daniel 5.** Chapter 5 tells the famous "handwriting on the wall" story.

■ **Daniel 5:1.** Belshazzar is the ruler in Babylon when the city falls to Darius (vv. 30-31). Verse 2 says that Nebuchadnezzar is Belshazzar's father. Babylonian sources name Nabonidus as Belshazzar's literal father. However, Nebuchadnezzar may have been Belshazzar's grandfather or great-grandfather. In Semitic languages, *father* may refer to one's actual father, to a grandfather, to a remote ancestor, or to a predecessor in office.

Belshazzar was apparently co-regent with Nabonidus for a time. Babylonian texts state that Nabonidus entrusted Belshazzar with "kingship." This was in 550 or 549 BC, at the beginning of Nabonidus's ten-year absence from Babylon.

According to the Nabonidus Chronicles, Nabonidus was not in Babylon when the city fell. He and his army had been defeated at Sippur and were in flight from the Persian army. He later returned to Babylon and was arrested.

The classical Greek writers, Herodotus and Zenophon, tell of a feast in Babylon on the night of its fall. Herodotus cites this feast, as well as the poor communication within the vast city, as factors in its fall.

■ **Daniel 5:10-16.** The queen is not Belshazzar's wife, but the queen mother. She is Nitocris, Nebuchadnezzar's widow and Belshazzar's grandmother. She advises Belshazzar to call on Daniel for an interpretation. She praises Daniel's abilities as if Belshazzar does not know who he is. Yet, as the chief prefect (2:48) of Nebuchadnezzar's time, Daniel should have been known to Belshazzar.

Belshazzar had, in a sense, challenged the God of Israel with his use of the Temple vessels. Now that his challenge has been answered, perhaps he is afraid and does not truly want an interpretation. Perhaps Daniel's position and power had declined after Nebuchadnezzar's death.

- **Daniel 5:17-28.** Daniel reads the writing on the wall (v. 25) and interprets it (vv. 26-28). He also tells the king why the writing appeared (vv. 18-24).
- **Daniel 5:30-31.** Belshazzar died on the night of October 11, 539 BC.

Scholars have debated the precise identity of Darius the Mede through the years. No record of a person by this name has been found outside of Daniel. (He is not Darius I, king of Persia [522–486 BC]). He may have been the general who took Babylon for Cyrus, the king of Persia. Such a general is known, but by the name Gubaru.

Cuneiform economic texts tell of Cyrus's first two years of rule over Babylonia. Cyrus did not assume the title King of Babylon until some months after Babylon was taken. Until that time, he carried the title King of Lands. Thereafter, he was known by both titles. Gubaru died the year after Babylon fell.

Thus, Darius the Mede may have been a vassal king under Cyrus the Persian.

- **Daniel 6:14-18.** The king cares for Daniel more than the law. In his heart, he wants to save Daniel but is trapped by his own shortsightedness. In the end, he looks to God to deliver Daniel. Darius appears to believe in the power of Daniel's God to save him. He also recognizes Daniel's faithfulness. Darius realizes he has nothing to gain and much to lose if Daniel dies.
- **Daniel 6:19-24.** Darius's question to Daniel in verse 20 is a confession. He confesses that Daniel faithfully serves a living God in the face of human death. He also confesses that only God can change death into life.

Daniel is now able to testify to his innocence. Because he is blameless, God sent an angel to save him (as in 3:28). The writer of Hebrews (Hebrews 11:33) attributes Daniel's salvation to faith. Daniel's faith manifests in his blameless conduct before God and before Darius. His faith is vindicated in his rescue.

Darius is not punished, though he is not totally innocent of the wrong done Daniel. As in the stories in chapters 3, 4, and 5, human evil is followed by a revelation of God's nature and of God's power.

- **Daniel 7:1.** This verse is in the third person. The rest of the chapter is in the first person. This introduction presents the chapter as developing in two stages. First, Daniel wrote down his dream/vision. Second, this introduction was added and the report collected with other stories into the Book of Daniel.

Soon after assuming power, Nabonidus "bestowed kingship" on Belshazzar, sometime between 554 and 549 BC. Nabonidus then left on a long journey. He was absent from Babylon on ten successive new years. He traveled into and looked after the western regions of his empire.

- **Daniel 7:2-8.** Daniel describes the four beasts of his vision.
- **Daniel 7:2-3.** The "four winds of heaven" and the "great sea" place the vision on a cosmic scale. The sea is similar to the primordial deep out of which supernatural forces of destruction arise (Amos 7:4; Psalm 74:13). The beasts are primeval representations of human power, destruction, and evil. These beasts also represent four kings, though their specific identities are not given (v. 17).
- **Daniel 7:9-10.** The "Ancient of Days" is God, who is the first and the last (Isaiah 44:6). The thrones are for God and the heavenly court, or for God and the "one like a son of man" (v. 13). Fire is often associated with a theophany (Genesis 15:17; Exodus 3:2; Ezekiel 1:4) and with divine judgment (Revelation 4:5; Psalm 50:3).

Judgment is to be rendered in a formal court session. The record books are opened. Judgment is carried out according to what the books reveal. Books in which human deeds are recorded are known in Israel (Psalm 56:8-9; Isaiah 65:6) as well as in Egypt and Babylon.

- **Daniel 8.** Daniel has another vision, in which he is transported to Susa. This vision of a ram and a goat (representing Persia and Greece) also uses the symbolism of horns to represent sinful and rebellious leaders who will oppress the people of God and come under divine judgment. The heavenly messenger in this vision is named as Gabriel.
- **Daniel 8:9-12.** The small horn that grows is probably Antiochus IV (175–164 BC) He was a Seleucid descendant of one of the generals who took power at Alexander's death.

The "Beautiful Land" is Israel.

In growing toward heaven, this monarch seeks equality with God. The "host of the heavens" or "starry host" may be the faithful people of Israel. Or they may be other monarchs who also seek God-like power.

The "commander of the army of the LORD" ("prince of the host" in the NRSV) is the Lord God of hosts. Under Antiochus's rule, offerings to God in the Temple were outlawed and suspended for three years. The Temple was desecrated and Antiochus set up an altar to Zeus over the altar of burnt offering. This defiled altar is probably the "abomination that causes desolation" of Daniel 11:31 and the "rebellion that causes desolation" of 8:13.

The noun translated "people" in verse 12 may also mean "army."

DIMENSION THREE: WHAT DOES THE BIBLE MEAN TO ME?

Daniel 6—Freedom and Bondage

Chapter 6 is probably one of the most familiar stories in the Old Testament. The story of Daniel in the lions' den shows God's promise to deliver from certain death those who are faithful to God. The chapter ends with Darius's confession that God is "the living God / and he endures forever." In the mind of Darius, Daniel was saved by God because he was obedient to God.

HUMAN DESTINY, DIVINE CONTROL

Does obedience to God free us from worldly tyranny? We are not likely to be ordered to worship an idol. What kinds of tyranny do we face today that might lead us to disobey God's laws? Does obedience to God always save us from literal death as it did Daniel? Does obedience free us from fear of consequences? If so, how?

Daniel 7–8—Vision as Revelation

These two chapters describe for us a series of visions. Daniel sees four beasts that collectively represent God's judgment. Then he sees a vision of a ram and a goat. This latter vision concerns the kingdoms of Persia and Greece, as was stated in Dimension Two.

A vision from God carries revelation of the divine nature and of God's redemptive purposes and actions. If this is so, what do Daniel's visions in chapters 7–8 reveal about God? What do they reveal about God's redemptive purposes and actions?

Do you agree that the visions have proven true in some ways, but also hold the promise of more complete fulfillment? How were they fulfilled? What is yet to be fulfilled?

GENESIS to REVELATION **DANIEL**

At that time your people—everyone whose name is found written in the book—will be delivered. (12:1)

13

THE TIME OF THE END

Daniel 9–12

DIMENSION ONE: WHAT DOES THE BIBLE SAY?

Answer these questions by reading Daniel 9

1. What does Daniel study? (9:2)

2. How does Daniel respond to what he learns? (9:3)

3. What does Daniel confess to God? (9:4-15)

4. What does Daniel ask of God? (9:17-19)

5. Why does Gabriel come to Daniel? (9:22-23)

6. What does Gabriel tell Daniel? (9:24-27)

THE TIME OF THE END

Answer these questions by reading Daniel 10

7. When does this last great vision come to Daniel? (10:1, 4)

8. Who does Daniel see in this vision? (10:5-6)

9. Why does the man come to Daniel? (10:11-12)

10. What will the man make Daniel understand? (10:14)

11. How does the man help Daniel? (10:19)

12. What does the man reveal to Daniel from the Book of Truth? (10:21)

Answer these questions by reading Daniel 11

13. Of which kings does the man first speak? (11:2-4)

14. From what country is "the king of the South"? (11:5-8)

15. Who finally defeats the king of the South? (11:11-17)

16. Who takes over the kingdom of the North? (11:21)

17. Instead of defeating the South again, what does he do? (11:31)

18. How are the people divided by his actions? (11:32)

19. What does the king do until the "time of wrath is completed"? (11:36)

20. What will happen to this king? (11:45)

Answer these questions by reading Daniel 12

21. Who will arise after this? (12:1)

22. After a time of distress, what will happen? (12:1)

23. What is Daniel to do with the words he receives? Why? (12:4, 9)

24. When will these words be completed? (12:7)

25. Who will understand what is to happen? (12:10)

DIMENSION TWO: WHAT DOES THE BIBLE MEAN?

■ **Daniel 9:1-2.** The first year of Darius's reign was around 539 BC.

Daniel has access to books containing the word of the Lord to Jeremiah. He refers specifically to Jeremiah 25:11-12 (from 605 BC) and to Jeremiah 29:10. Jeremiah 29:10 is part of a copy of a letter Jeremiah wrote to the exiles in Babylon.

"Seventy years" may be a ritual number of years in which God's punishment of Israel is worked out (see Zechariah 1:12; 2 Chronicles 36:21).

■ **Daniel 9:4-6.** Daniel confesses that God is great and awesome, loyal and loving toward those who are faithful (Deuteronomy 7:9). He also confesses Israel's disloyalty. Including himself among the wrongdoers, he confirms the charges made by Ezekiel. Israel is rebellious and disobedient.

■ **Daniel 9:7-10.** God is righteous, merciful, and forgiving. Israel is confused, or literally "covered with shame" (v. 7) and guilty (see Ezra 9:5-7).

■ **Daniel 9:11-14.** Through the "curses and sworn judgments" (v. 11; see Leviticus 26:14-39; Deuteronomy 28:15-45), God warned Israel of the consequences of disobedience. The "Law of Moses, the servant of God" (v. 11) records this warning (Joshua 1:1; 8:31; 1 Kings 2:3).

Daniel proclaims the prophetic "therefore" (v. 11; see Ezekiel 14:3-4), convicting Israel and justifying its punishment.

■ **Daniel 9:15-16.** Daniel reminds God of God's mighty act of salvation in the Exodus. The Exodus established God's fame among the other nations, even up to Daniel's day. Daniel yearns for a new Exodus in which the exiles may return to Jerusalem. He pleads with God to act in light of God's past saving activities toward Israel, not in light of what Israel deserves.

■ **Daniel 9:17-19.** Verse 19 summarizes Daniel's supplications to God. He asks God to hear his confession of sin, forgive the sin, and act on behalf of God's city and people.

Jerusalem and the people of Israel are identified with God's name. Their salvation would vindicate God's name before the nations.

■ **Daniel 9:26.** The "ruler who will come" may be Antiochus IV. He came to power in 175 BC.

The "Anointed One" who "will be put to death" may be Onias III. He was high priest in Jerusalem until Antiochus deposed him; he was assassinated in 171 BC.

The "people of the ruler" are his army. Antiochus's forces sacked Jerusalem and set it on fire. They did not completely destroy the city or the Temple. The Romans destroyed the Temple in AD 70.

"A flood" may be a figure of speech for divine punishment.

The "end" is the time appointed for the end of this prince and his desolations (v. 27).

■ **Daniel 9:27.** Here Gabriel is talking about the prince. During one "seven" he will enjoy power. Sacrifice and offering in the Temple will cease for half of this "seven."

The last part of verse 27 is not entirely clear. It could also be translated as "At the corner (of the altar) will be an appalling abomination." Here, the word "temple" (or "wing," see footnote) may also mean the pinnacle of the Temple (Matthew 4:5). This word may refer to the altar to Zeus that Antiochus put on top of the altar of burnt offering in the Temple.

This reference may also point to another one to come after the prince who makes "a covenant." This leader brings desolation to God's people. Regardless of the precise identity, the end of the abomination is set and decreed by God.

Identifying the historical situations spoken by Gabriel is difficult. These numbers could be symbolic. The different stages in human history serve as signposts for God's people. Such signposts help them recognize God's plan as it unfolds. These signs also point the people to God's future plan for them. The important message here is that, though suffering is inevitable, an end to suffering is also inevitable for God's people.

THE TIME OF THE END

■ **Daniel 10:4-6.** The first Hebrew month is Nisan (parts of our March and April). Daniel apparently had been mourning for three weeks prior to the twenty-fourth and did not celebrate Passover. Passover begins on the fifteenth day of Nisan.

The appearance of the man Daniel sees is similar to that of the celestial being seen by Ezekiel (Ezekiel 1:7, 13, 26-28; 9:2).

■ **Daniel 10:7-9.** Daniel's natural beauty and grace, or vigor, and his strength were drained at the sight of the heavenly messenger.

■ **Daniel 10:10-14.** Daniel mourned in order to humble himself before God and to gain understanding from God. For this reason the man comes to him.

The prince (v. 13) is the patron angel of Persia. Michael is the patron angel of Israel (12:1). As a chief prince, he is one of the archangels that stand closer to the divine throne than other angels. Earthly conflict is mirrored in heavenly conflict between the patron angels (see also v. 20).

The future (v. 14) involves a resolution of God's promises to Israel for restoration. This image includes the promises of Daniel 9:24. It also anticipates the end of the age when the kingdom of the saints is fully realized (7:27).

■ **Daniel 11:3-4.** The vision is told in the future tense.

Alexander the Great is the mighty king. His kingdom stretched from the Adriatic through the Near East to India. He died at the height of his power in 323 BC. His kingdom was divided among four of his generals, who did not have his power (Daniel 8:22). His two sons were murdered thirteen years after his death.

■ **Daniel 11:5-6.** The "South" is Egypt, the kingdom of Ptolemy I (306–285 BC). Ptolemy began his reign stronger than Seleucus I, another of Alexander's generals who was satrap over Babylonia and controlled the Northern Kingdom. Seleucus fled to Egypt for political reasons and was made a general in Ptolemy's army. With Egyptian military help, he regained control of the North. He eventually extended his rule from Asia Minor to the Indies.

Around 250 BC, Ptolemy II of Egypt gave his daughter, Bernice, in marriage to Antiochus II of Syria (the Northern Kingdom was centered in Syria). Antiochus II, Bernice, and their son were murdered by Laodice, Antiochus's ex-wife, so that her son, Seleucus II, could assume the throne.

■ **Daniel 11:11-12.** Antiochus III (223–187 BC) attacked Ptolemy IV in 217 BC, and was defeated. Ptolemy did not follow up his advantage. He signed a peace agreement with Antiochus.

■ **Daniel 11:13.** In 205 BC, fresh from conquests in Persia, Antiochus III moved against Ptolemy V (four-year-old son of Ptolemy IV) in Phoenicia, Syria, and Gaza.

■ **Daniel 11:22-24.** The "prince of the covenant" (v. 22) may be the high priest Onias III. Antiochus IV made an alliance with Jason, a Jewish leader who paid Antiochus a large sum in order to be appointed high priest. Antiochus was a deceitful schemer, however. He deposed Jason in favor of Menelaus, who paid him an even larger sum. Menelaus was supported by part of the Jewish community in Jerusalem, though he allowed his troops to plunder Judah.

■ **Daniel 11:25-28.** These verses describe Antiochus's campaign against Egypt in 170 BC. The king of the South is Ptolemy VI (Philometor), Antiochus's nephew. Ptolemy was defeated, in part by traitors in his own camp. Antiochus IV captured him; then his brother, Ptolemy Physcon, assumed the Egyptian throne. Antiochus and Ptolemy Philometor used one another to try to recapture Egypt, but failed.

Antiochus IV returned to his homeland with spoils from Egypt. On the way, he sacked Jerusalem and carried away some of the Temple treasury.

■ **Daniel 12:4.** As in 8:26, Daniel is to put away what he has seen, heard, and recorded "until the time of the end." "Many will go here and there," seeking knowledge of God's word (see Amos 8:12). Knowledge will increase, perhaps because of this earnest seeking.

Daniel's book might have been hidden away until the end of the reign of Antiochus IV. Obviously, it has not been hidden away until the end of all things. The shutting-up may be figurative, in the sense that the end is fixed or sealed by God.

■ **Daniel 12:5-7.** Two more angels appear. The man raises both of his hands toward heaven as a gesture to call heaven to witness to the truth of his oath (Deuteronomy 32:40).

■ **Daniel 12:8-10.** Daniel is told to go on with his life. By implication, he is told not to question what is beyond him.

Those who are purified and refined may be the martyrs in the fight for righteousness (Daniel 11:35; Revelation 6:11).

The wicked, whether Jew or non-Jew, will continue in their ways because they do not understand that God is in control. The wise understand this, even though they may not understand all the details of God's plan.

DIMENSION THREE: WHAT DOES THE BIBLE MEAN TO ME?

The End Time and the Meantime

After studying the Book of Daniel for the past three lessons, you are aware that this biblical book contains words pertaining to the end of time. So also does the Book of Ezekiel. Perhaps during this entire unit of study you have done more reflection about the end of time than you normally do.

How does knowledge of the end of time affect the way we live now? How has your concept of the end of time changed as a result of this study of Ezekiel and Daniel?

Jesus proclaimed that "the gates of Hades will not overcome" God's church (Matthew 16:18). Does Daniel also give us this same message? Does this knowledge encourage you to offer courageous, confident service to God? Why or why not?

Daniel 10–12—Daniel and the Future

These three chapters in Daniel are a vision of the end of time. Chapter 10 serves as an introduction to the vision itself, which is found in chapter 11. Following the vision, there is an interpretation of the vision, which takes up most of chapter 12.

The vision of Daniel 10–12 may apply to the restoration of Israel following the overthrow of Antiochus IV. The vision may also foreshadow even more distant future events. Jesus applied some of Daniel's prophecy in this way (Matthew 24:15-28; Mark 13).

What parts of the Book of Daniel have you had the most difficulty understanding? Why? What questions still remain in your mind after completing your study of Daniel?

What is the most important thing you have learned from Daniel?

GLOSSARY

Abednego: (uh-BED-ni-goh) Daniel's companion. Cast into the fiery furnace with Shadrach and Meshach.

Akkadian: (uh-KAY-dee-uhn) People from the region between the Tigris and Euphrates rivers.

Amasis: Took the Egyptian throne from Hophra following a revolt.

Ammonites: (AM-uh-nightz) Semitic nomads descended from Ammon.

Antiochus IV: (an-TIGH-uh-kuhs) One of the cruelest Greek tyrants. Ravaged Jerusalem.

Arameans: (air-uh-MEE-uhns) People who occupied the region of Aram, north of Palestine.

Asher: (ASH-uhr) One of the twelve tribes, descended from the eighth son of Jacob.

Bamah: (BAY-muh) High place.

Bastet: (BAS-tet) An Egyptian goddess.

Belshazzar: (bel-SHAZ-uhr) The firstborn son and coregent of Nabonidus, the last king of the Neo-Babylonian Empire.

Bilhah: (BIL-huh) The mother of Dan and Naphtali; a servant of Jacob's wife Rachel.

Cappadocia: (kap-uh-DOH-shee-uh) A highland province in eastern Asia Minor.

Carchemish: (KAHR-kuh-mish) The capital of the Hittites. Neco, king of Egypt, was defeated by Nebuchadnezzar here.

Chaldea: (kal-DEE-uh) A large area of Babylonia.

Chaldeans: (kal-DEE-uhnz) People who lived in south Babylonia. Also refers to the last dynasty of Babylonia (629–539 BC).

Chebar: (KEE-bahr) River where Ezekiel had his prophetic visions.

Cunieform: (kyoo-NEE-uh-form) An ancient style of writing.

Darius: (duh-RIGH-uhs) Leader of the Medes. Mentioned in the Book of Daniel.

Diblah: (DIB-luh) A city on the Orontes River, north of the boundary of Israel and Syria. "Riblah" in NRSV.

Edom: (EE-duhm) The land and people who were neighbors of Israelites to the south and east.

Ephraim: (EE-fray-im) One of the twelve tribes, one of Joseph's sons.

Gabriel: (GAY-bree-uhl) Angel who helps Daniel.

Gedaliah: (ged-uh-LIGH-uh) The exilic governor of Jerusalem and Judah under Nebuchadnezzar.

Haggai: (HAG-igh) Tenth of the Minor Prophets.

Hophra: (HOF-ruh) Egyptian pharaoh.

Issachar: (IS-uh-kahr) One of the twelve tribes, descended from the ninth son of Jacob.

Javan: (JAY-vuhn) Region in Asia Minor; descendants of Japheth (Genesis 10:2).

Jebusite: (JEB-yoo-site) A tribe of people that inhabited Canaan before the Hebrews.

GLOSSARY

Jehoiachin: (Ji-HOY-uh-kin) The son and successor of Jehoiakim.

Jehoiakim: (Ji-HOY-uh-kim) King of Judah 609–598 BC. Son of Josiah.

Kabod: (kuh-BODE) The Hebrew word for the glory of God.

Laodice: (luh-OH-dih-say) Wife of Antiochus II.

Meshach: (MEE-shak) Daniel's companion; thrown into the fiery furnace with Shadrach and Abednego.

Meshech: (MEH-shek) Region in Asia Minor; descendants of Japheth (Genesis 10:2).

Mesopotamia: (mes-uh-puh-TAY-mee-uh) The land between the Tigris and Euphrates rivers. Some exiles are sent here.

Moab: (MOH-ab) An area east of the Dead Sea and south of the Jordan River.

Nabonidus: (nab-uh-NIGH-duhs) Last king of the Neo-Babylonian (Chaldean) Empire.

Nabopolossar: (nab-uh-puh-LAS-uhr) Nebuchadnezzar's father.

Naphtali: (NAF-tuh-ligh) One of the twelve tribes, descended from the sixth son of Jacob.

Nebuchadnezzar, Nebuchadrezzar: (neb-uh-kuhd-NEZ-uhr; neb-uhkuh-DREZ-uhr) King of Babylon (605–562 BC)

Negev: (NEG-ev) Grazing region a few miles south of Hebron.

Nisan: (NIGH-san) The first month of the year in the Hebrew calendar.

Oholah: (oh-HOH-luh) Sister of Oholibah in Ezekiel's allegory.

Oholibah: (oh-HOH-lee-ba) Sister of Oholah in Ezekiel's allegory.

Onias III: (oh-NIGH-uhs) A high priest.

Pelatiah: (pel-uh-TIGH-uh) A prince of Israel who misled the people. Ezekiel prophesied against him.

Pelusium: (pi-LOO-see-uhm) A place on the Nile River.

Philistia: (fil-US-tee-uh) The land of the Philistines.

Philometor: (fil-uh-MEE-tor) A king of Egypt ("the South"), Ptolemy VI.

Pi-beseth: (pigh-BEE-sith) An Egyptian city named after a goddess.

Polytheist: (POL-ee-thee-ist) Believer in the existence of more than one god.

Ptolemy: (TOL-uh-mee) The name of all male Egyptian rulers from the time of Alexander the Great until the Roman Empire.

Riblah: (RIB-luh) City in the land of Hamath. Nebuchadnezzar was camped there when Zedekiah was captured and blinded. Also see *Diblah*.

Satrap: (SA-trup) Official title of governors of Persian provinces.

Seleucus: (si-LOO-kuhs) A king of Syria.

Senir: (SEE-nuhr) Amorite name of Mount Hermon.

Shadrach: (SHAD-rak) Companion to Daniel; cast into the fiery furnace with Meshach and Abednego.

GLOSSARY

Sidon: (SIGH-duhn) An ancient Canaanite city.

Tahpanhes: (TAH-puh-neez) Egyptian city where some exiles lived.

Tahmud: (TAL-mood) Book of Jewish law.

Tehaphnehes: (tuh-HAF-nuh-heez) Egyptian city where some exiles lived.

Thebes: (theebz) An Egyptian city.

Theophany: (thee-OF-uh-nee) The appearance of God to humans.

Tubal: (TOO-buhl) Region in Asia Minor; descendants of Japheth (Genesis 10:2).

Tyre: (tire) An important Phoenician seaport.

Uphaz: (YOO-faz) A place where gold was bought.

Zadokites: (ZAY-duh-kightz) Priests given control of the Temple.

Zebulun: (ZEB-yuh-luhn) One of the twelve tribes, descended from the tenth son of Jacob.

Zedekiah: (zed-uh-KIGH-uh) The last king of Judah.

Zephaniah: (zef-uh-NIGH-uh) A Judean prophet, ninth book of the Minor Prophets.

Zilphah: (ZIL-puh) The mother of Gad and Asher; a servant of Jacob's wife Leah.

About the Writer

Linda B. Hinton wrote this study book on Ezekiel and Daniel. Ms. Hinton graduated from the Candler School of Theology, Emory University, with a Master of Theological Studies. Her field is Old Testament studies.

www.ingramcontent.com/pod-product-compliance
Lightning Source LLC
LaVergne TN
LVHW061254060426
835507LV00020B/2319